# The Panic Attack Relief Workbook

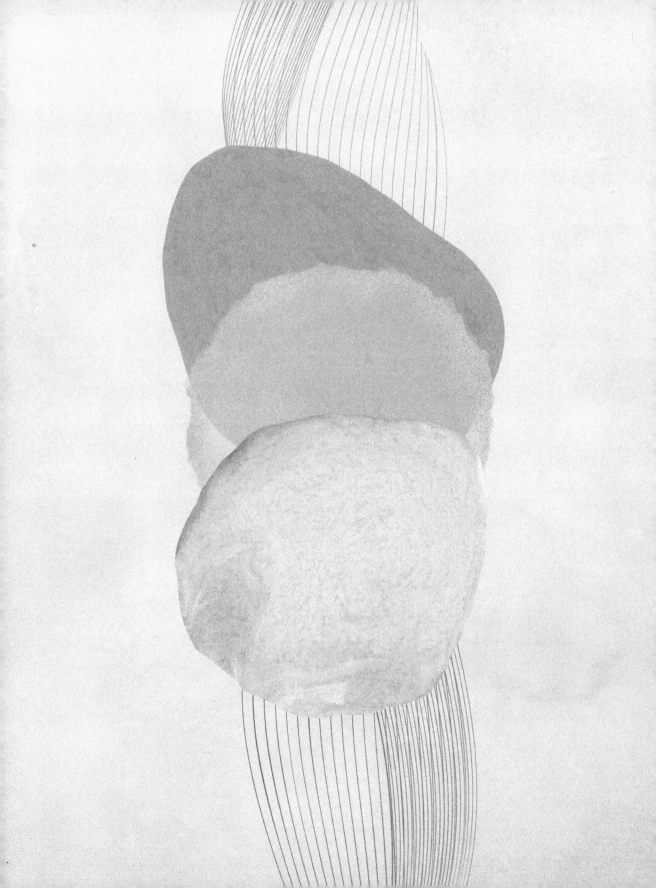

# THE
# Panic Attack Relief
## WORKBOOK

A 7-Week Plan for Overcoming Fear,
Managing Panic, and Finding Calm

Mayra Diaz, MS, LMFT

ROCKRIDGE
PRESS

First Rockridge Press trade paperback edition 2022



For general information on our other products and services, please contact our Customer Care Department within the United States at (866) 744-2665, or outside the United States at (510) 253-0500.

Paperback ISBN: 978-1-63807-795-4 | eBook ISBN: 978-1-68539-125-6

Manufactured in the United States of America

Interior and Cover Designer: John Calmeyer
Art Producer: Samantha Ulban
Editor: Mo Mozuch
Production Editor: Nora Milman
Production Manager: Lanore Coloprisco

All images used under license © Lisima/Creative Market.
Author photo courtesy of Baha Danesh.

10 9 8 7 6 5 4 3 2 1 0

# CONTENTS

# INTRODUCTION

've had one panic attack in my life, and it was horrifying. I was on the floor of a bathroom stall, sobbing, feeling like everything was absolutely awful and I could do nothing to fix it. It had been a long day. It started with a 6:30 a.m. work shift, included a couple midterms, and ended around midnight. I had a cold and felt jittery all day. My nervous system was strung out on caffeine, very little sleep, and cold medicine.

On my way home from my late-night studying, a stranger T-boned me on my bike. It was a very mild accident. I didn't even hit the ground, just went spinning in the opposite direction. But with all the stress I had been keeping at bay, my body was pushed past its limits; it was the last straw. I rushed into a nearby bathroom, feeling tears stinging my eyes, and hoping no one I knew was in the building. Then I collapsed. It felt like I was being pressed in from all sides, like my whole body was vibrating.

Thankfully, that was the result of external factors I could easily recognize. I never again mixed excessive amounts of caffeine with cold medicine, and I tried to respect the limits of my body better. It's not perfect. I still struggle with anxiety, but I've never felt that overwhelming loss of control again. So, when I say I understand what you're going through, I want you to know I mean it.

I've been helping people take their lives back from anxiety for almost a decade now. I love working with anxiety because it makes sense. I've learned that most struggles with anxiety don't come from "broken" nervous systems or deep, mysterious issues but instead from a lack of understanding. Most of us were not taught how our bodies operate and why they do things that seem so frightening or confusing, or how our thoughts and behaviors interact with our experience of anxiety.

You don't have to be afraid of your body. You don't have to feel paralyzed by your panic. But you do need to learn your own cycle and how to have a healthy relationship with anxiety. This workbook will teach you how to understand your panic so that you can manage it.

However, if you feel your panic is negatively impacting your life in significant ways that you are still struggling to handle, please reach out to a health-care professional. Ideally, seek out a specialist in anxiety who will know how to support your specific needs. This book can't be a replacement for the care of a therapist or medical doctor. Be your own best support by giving yourself permission to get the help you deserve.

# HOW TO USE THIS BOOK

Dealing with panic takes work. But if you do the work, you can develop a deep understanding of yourself and confidence in your ability to handle challenges. It will take bravery, commitment, and a willingness to be vulnerable. You will struggle, but that's normal. I will use case studies to help you see you are not alone and give you examples of how others have successfully managed their panic. Through prompts, exercises, practices, and affirmations, you will learn strategies to effectively tackle your panic.

In part 1, you will come to understand the roots of your panic. You will learn how to spot a panic attack, including the physical symptoms and the science of what is going on in your body. You will also learn about how excessive panic can lead to mental health issues, where panic comes from, and common triggers for panic attacks. This part also covers therapeutic treatment options, lifestyle changes, and practices to alleviate panic. Last, I will introduce you to your seven-week plan to manage panic.

In part 2, you will put the seven-week plan into action. Each week will build on the next. Learning how to manage your panic involves actively practicing awareness of your body, your thoughts, and your behaviors. It is also essential to learn effective tools to reframe distorted thoughts and confront your fears. You will learn these skills throughout the seven weeks.

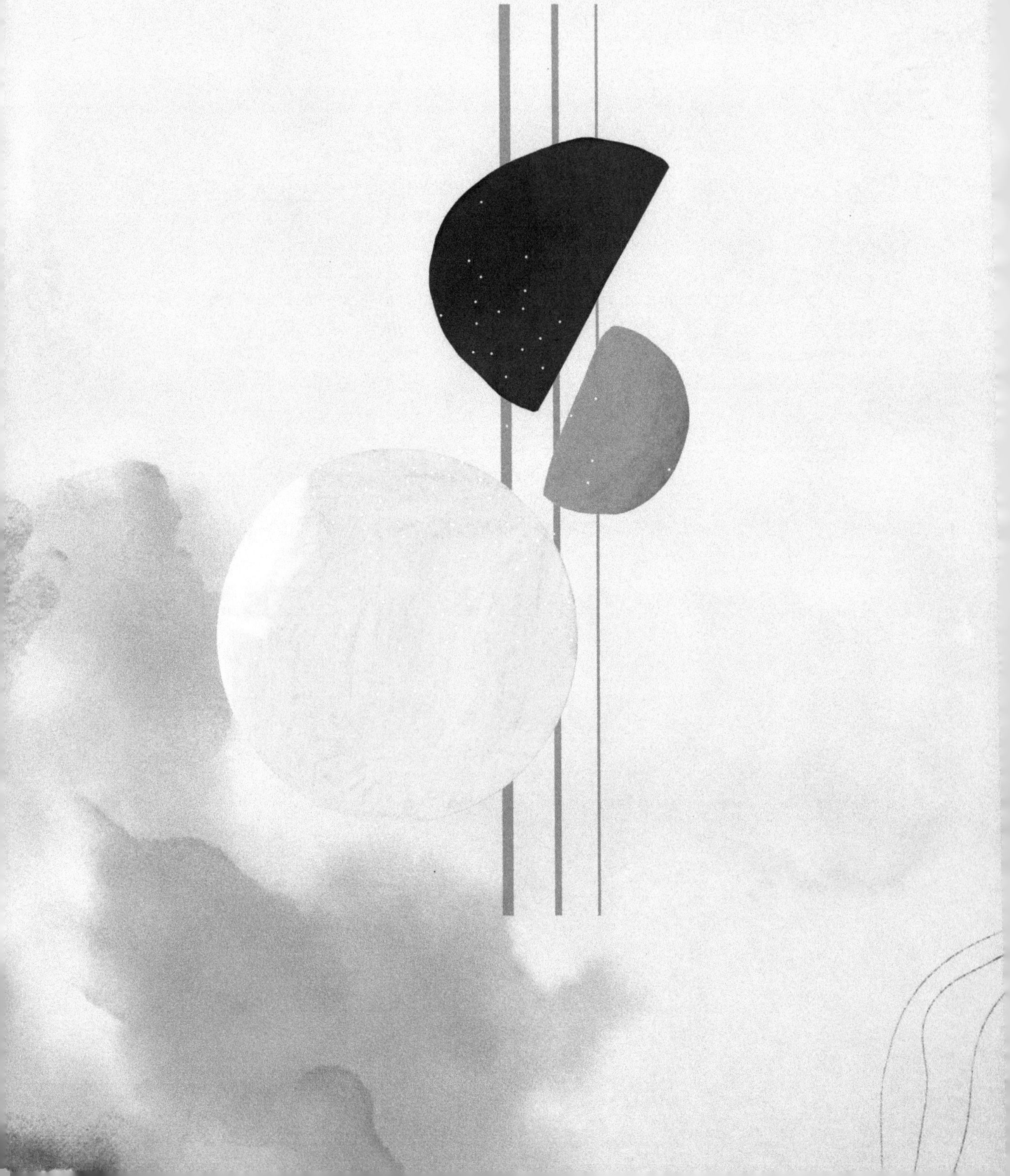

# *an*
# INTRODUCTION
## *to*
# PANIC ATTACKS

Understanding the science around panic is crucial to stop panic from controlling your life. This part will teach you why we experience panic and what causes attacks. You will learn the signs and symptoms of panic attacks to better understand what triggers yours. You will learn about different mental health issues related to panic and the influences that genetics and life experiences have on you. You will also learn what is happening in your brain and body during panic, and how anticipatory anxiety, trauma, and major life changes can trigger panic attacks.

This part also reviews evidence-based therapeutic treatment methods, including cognitive behavioral therapy (CBT), acceptance and commitment therapy (ACT), and exposure therapy. You will also learn about how mindfulness, medication, and lifestyle changes can alleviate panic attacks. This will help you tailor each step of your seven-week plan to meet your needs. Each chapter includes affirmations for you to use to support you on your journey. Repeat them to yourself or keep them posted somewhere visible as you work your way through this book.

*Panic is a normal human experience.*
*Everyone experiences anxiety and panic.*
*I am not alone.*

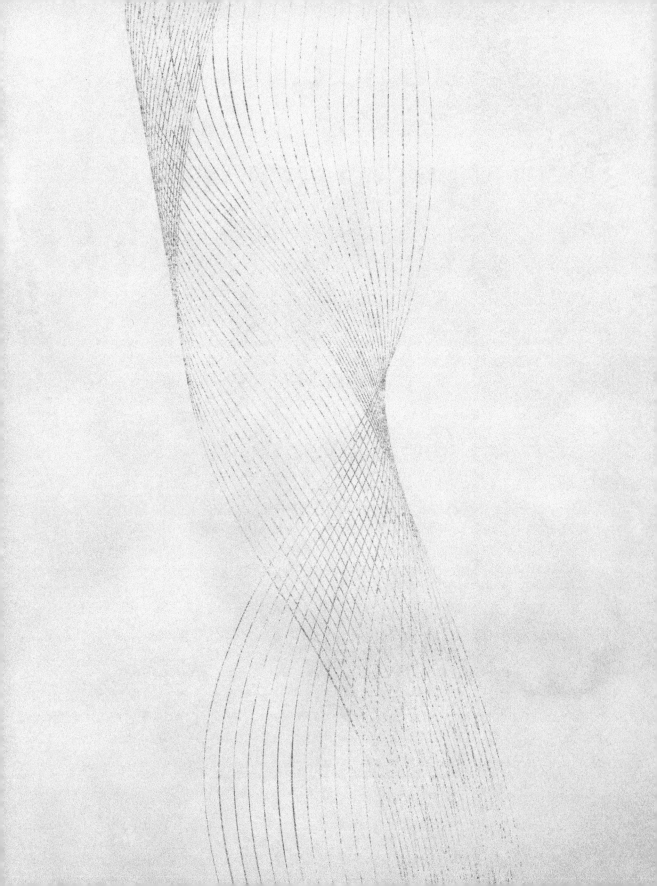

# CHAPTER ONE

# Understanding the Roots of Panic

Most people who have panic attacks are confused and upset about what they're experiencing. Not understanding what's happening in your body is a big part of what makes a panic attack scary. When you understand why your symptoms are happening, it will help you shift from feeling like a victim to being an objective observer. This understanding will also help you respond to distorted thoughts in a more helpful way.

This chapter teaches you where panic commonly comes from so you can understand some of your own root causes. You will learn about possible mental health issues you could be struggling with or factors that contribute to panic such as anticipatory anxiety, specific experiences that trigger fear, and major life stressors.

Panic causes a wide range of symptoms. It can look very different from how the media portrays it, and it can also be invisible to outsiders. Shortness of breath and sweaty palms are your panic trying to protect you. Symptoms like these are often the unintended consequences of targeted changes in your body, so we'll look at your nervous system and the neuroscience of what's going on in your brain. The goal is for you to make sense of what's happening in your body and understand what is contributing to your panic.

*I will learn about the science and the tools to deal with my panic in healthy ways.*

Victor had no idea what was happening. His head was between his knees, chest heaving. He was at his job at a busy restaurant during the dinner rush. He had been taking an order from a customer. The customer had been unhappy, snapping at him about a mistake and threatening to speak to his manager. Victor had already gotten one write-up this month because of excessive tardiness. He had a new baby and was finding it hard to get to work on time.

As the customer berated him, Victor felt his temperature rising. His cheeks started to burn, and he began to wonder if the customer could tell. Her voice was getting louder, and he worried that his manager would come out. His heart felt like it was leaping into his throat. He began to have trouble swallowing, like he didn't have enough saliva. He wondered how many write-ups he could get before his boss started to think he was unreliable. What if he was suspended? How would he be able to make rent next month? His wife was still on maternity leave, so they were counting on his income to pay the bills.

He started to feel nauseous and worried about getting sick in front of the customer. Victor excused himself, rushing to the storeroom. As the door swung shut, he felt like he couldn't breathe. He staggered to a chair, terrified and confused. He wondered if he was having a heart attack. He felt certain he was dying.

Victor ended up at an emergency room, desperate to see a cardiologist. The doctors ran several tests and told him his heart was fine. They asked if he'd ever had a panic attack before and recommended that he seek therapy to deal with his stress.

## What Are Panic Attacks?

Panic is an intense and rapid surge of fear or discomfort. *Fear* is our emotional response to an immediate threat (real or perceived). *Anxiety* is anticipation of a future threat. It builds more slowly and can last longer. "Anxiety attack" is actually a misnomer because anxiety does not cause an abrupt surge of fear. The correct term is "panic attack."

Many people think of panic attacks as being dramatic and impossible to miss; that's not necessarily true.

As defined by *The Diagnostic and Statistical Manual of Mental Disorders*, 5th edition, a panic attack has two requirements: (1) panic that peaks within minutes, paired with (2) four or more of the following symptoms:

- Heart pounding or racing

- Sweating

- Trembling or shaking

- Shortness of breath or feelings of being smothered

- Feelings of choking

- Chest pain or discomfort

- Nausea or upset stomach

- Feeling dizzy, unsteady, lightheaded, or faint

- Hot or cold flashes

- Paresthesia (numbness or tingling, especially in the hands or feet)

- Derealization (a surreal, "off" feeling)

- Depersonalization (feeling detached from yourself, including an out-of-body experience)

- Thinking you are losing control

- Thinking you are dying

- Thinking you are going crazy

So, yes, a panic attack can be obvious, but it can also be invisible. You could experience a rapid surge of fear and nausea, numbness, lightheadedness, and a sense of things seeming surreal—and no one would know you were having a panic attack. You can also have a limited symptom attack, which just means experiencing panic with fewer than four of the symptoms. Because there are so many symptoms that can happen during an attack, everyone's panic attacks look different. They may also look different for the same person from one attack to the next.

## How Panic Attacks Lead to Panic Disorder

Panic attacks are a common experience. According to the U.S. National Comorbidity Survey Replication, about 22 percent of Americans have experienced a panic attack in their lifetimes. This survey also found that 2.7 percent of Americans report experiencing panic disorder. That's *six million* people.

Having a panic attack by itself does not mean you are suffering from a mental illness. Panic disorder, however, is a formal diagnosis in *The Diagnostic and Statistical*

*Manual of Mental Disorders.* The criteria for panic disorder are experiencing repeated unexpected panic attacks, struggling for at least one month with persistent worry about having another panic attack, and/or a significant change in your behavior due to your panic attacks that is negatively impacting your life. Panic disorder is diagnosed by a health-care professional. To reach a diagnosis, your symptoms and family history will be assessed. Panic attacks share similar symptoms with other medical issues, so a doctor will also evaluate you for other physical causes to rule them out.

Panic disorder, a type of anxiety disorder, develops due to a fear of physical sensations associated with panic, which can be distressing. Over time, that distress can lead to avoidance. We can also experience symptoms related to panic—such as an increase in heart rate—at other times, such as when we're exercising. A fear of physiological symptoms can lead to avoidance of not just things that can cause panic but anything that brings up similar physical sensations. Avoidance actually worsens fear, supporting the belief that the thing we are avoiding (e.g., shortness of breath) is in fact dangerous. This creates a vicious cycle of escalating panic and increasing behaviors to prevent panic that only serve to exacerbate fear.

Experiencing panic is normal in threatening situations, like a hurricane or a car accident. Feeling like panic is taking over your life is a sign that you're dealing with something more serious and could use professional help.

# What Makes Panic Disorder Different from Other Issues?

You may experience panic attacks and be dealing with a different mental health issue. Generalized anxiety disorder (GAD) involves struggling to manage excessive worry about various things in your life and a high level of tension that leads to symptoms such as body aches, irritability, and trouble relaxing. This worry may lead to panic attacks, but they are not the sole cause of your panic attacks.

Obsessive compulsive disorder (OCD) involves obsessions, which are persistent, intrusive, distressing thoughts, images, or urges that lead to compulsions—repetitive, often ritualistic or excessive behaviors aimed at neutralizing the distress. Obsessions may lead to panic attacks, but the core feature of this disorder is the obsessive-compulsive cycle.

Post-traumatic stress disorder (PTSD) occurs after experiencing or having been exposed to actual or threatened death, serious injury, or sexual violence. This can cause intrusive symptoms such as flashbacks or nightmares, avoidance of trauma reminders, negative thoughts and feelings, and hyperarousal (an increased physical and emotional sensitivity). The hyperarousal and negative thoughts or feelings can lead to panic attacks as your body attempts to cope with the traumatic event.

Social anxiety disorder (SAD) is intense fear or anxiety of social situations where you may be judged by others, leading to avoidance of social activities. You can experience panic when struggling with social anxiety disorder, but it will be due to a fear of negative judgment. Similar to social anxiety disorder, a specific phobia indicates an intense and excessive fear of a particular situation or thing.

The fear of panic itself is the core feature of panic disorder that differentiates it from these other issues.

# Where Panic Comes From

We all feel panic on occasion. Panic exists to protect us from an immediate threat. Panic comes from our fight-or-flight response, the body's natural system that prepares us to run or face something we think is dangerous. Panic, even to the point of panic attacks, is not harmful in the short term. We need panic to marshal the body's resources to rush under a table during an earthquake or defend ourselves from an attacker. Panic is meant to flare up briefly in the moment of crisis and then subside when the danger has passed.

Panic becomes a problem when you experience it in situations that are not actually threatening and when the attacks become more and more frequent without any logical cause. Or when you become afraid of the symptoms of panic and start to change your life to avoid anything that reminds you of a panic attack, such as anything that might make your heart beat faster or your palms sweat. Panic leads to panic disorder when that fear of an attack has started to overwhelm you and control how you live.

There is no one specific cause for panic disorder. Likely, panic disorder arises from a combination of heritable genetic factors and life experiences. Let's take a look.

## GENETICS

Panic disorder has been shown to run in families. According to a meta-analysis of the genetic epidemiology of anxiety disorders in the *American Journal of Psychiatry*, the heritability of panic disorder is 43 percent. We don't currently have a clear reason why. There has been research into genes that are possibly associated with panic disorder, as well as research into genes that link anxiety and depression. However, at this time, there is no one gene we can point to that causes panic disorder. Likely, people inherit a sensitivity that makes them more susceptible to panic and other strong emotions.

## LIFESTYLE

Your life experiences and what you have learned impact your relationship to panic. Panic attacks are more likely to begin in a person's twenties, probably because that stage in life involves lots of changes and stressors. Research published in 2018 in *Social Psychiatry and Psychiatric Epidemiology* has shown that a traumatic experience leading to post-traumatic stress disorder could also lead to panic disorder. How we've learned to view the world from our peers or caregivers can also affect our experience of panic. Many people who struggle with panic attacks have learned to be afraid of their physical symptoms, such as a fear that heart palpitations mean they are having a heart attack or strong emotions mean they are going insane or losing control.

# What Causes Panic Attacks?

At its most basic, we feel panic because we perceive there is an immediate danger. There are some things, through evolution, that we have been predisposed to be anxious about, such as spiders or animals with big fangs. This innate anxiety may lead to a phobia if we lived through an experience that spiked that anxiety into fear, like being bitten by a dog.

It is important to note that we only need to *think* something is dangerous for panic to be activated. Our mind may perceive something as dangerous even if it isn't, possibly because of our beliefs or lived experiences. Those thoughts can lead to anticipatory anxiety, a prolonged and intense sense of dread about what may come. This anxiety can then feed back into panic, causing a person to avoid situations related to panic and thus continuing to reinforce the belief that the trigger they are avoiding is dangerous. Stress itself can cause panic, even good stress due to a promotion or buying a new house.

### ANTICIPATORY ANXIETY

Anxiety feels similar to fear and originates from the same place panic does: the nervous system. Anticipation arises from the brain's ability to prepare for the future by processing or visualizing it. Anticipatory anxiety is the sense of dread we feel when we anticipate a future event we interpret as threatening. Panic is a scary and uncomfortable experience. So, it makes sense that someone who went through a panic attack would try to anticipate situations that would trigger another attack to prevent it from happening. That anticipation can cause a stress response as strong as if we were experiencing our fear in the moment, causing and feeding into panic.

### SPECIFIC PHOBIAS

A phobia is an intense fear of a specific object or situation that is more extreme than the trigger warrants. Phobias can arise when a fear that has been programmed into us by evolution is paired with an experience that causes intense discomfort in the moment, like falling from a tree and breaking your arm. Phobias can also develop because you experienced panic once in an incredibly frightening event. If you got into a car accident that terrified you at the time, you may start to associate that fear with driving. You might avoid driving altogether, reinforcing that fear and, over time, developing a trigger for panic attacks.

## MAJOR LIFE CHANGES AND TRAUMA

A stressor is anything that pushes your body out of its sense of balance. Your stress response is what your body does to bring itself back to balance, which can put a strain on your system and make you more likely to panic. Major life changes like a new baby or traumatic experiences like an auto accident cause stress. When you experience stress, you also experience muscle tension. That tension can impact your ability to think and distort your view of the world, possibly making everything seem more threatening or extreme. To cope, you might start avoiding entire activities, like work functions or crowded places, again reinforcing triggers for panic.

## When Agoraphobia Enters the Mix

Agoraphobia is the intense fear of having a panic attack or embarrassing symptoms (like getting sick to your stomach) in a situation where escape would be difficult or help may not be available. This fear leads people to avoid those situations, such as movie theaters or traveling far from home, in a way that starts to significantly impact their life. Severe agoraphobia may prevent someone from leaving their house at all. But you can also have agoraphobia if you only avoid certain situations, like the place you had your first attack.

According to the National Comorbidity Survey Replication, agoraphobia affects about 2 percent of the U.S. population. It is most common among women and occurs in higher numbers among teenagers and the elderly. Panic disorder can exist without agoraphobia, and agoraphobia can exist with or without panic disorder. If someone avoids situations where there may not be a restroom for fear of having an accident because of incontinence or nausea, with no experience of panic attacks, that would be an example of agoraphobia without panic disorder.

I describe living with agoraphobia as though your whole life is narrowing. Over time, there are fewer and fewer places or activities you engage in for fear of experiencing uncomfortable symptoms. Agoraphobia can limit you from the things you want to do or make it hard to be in the moment when you are doing things you usually enjoy. But it can be overcome. The tools you learn here can help you face what you've been avoiding and get back to your normal life.

# The Science of a Panic Attack

When your mind registers something threatening, it relays that message of danger to your autonomic nervous system. Your autonomic nervous system is made up of two subsystems: your sympathetic nervous system (SNS) and your parasympathetic nervous system (PNS). These systems control your body's energy levels and either spark your body into action or bring it back to a resting state.

Panic originates from your SNS. You can think of your SNS as the gas pedal, igniting your panic or anxiety, and your PNS as the brake, slowing your body back down. Your SNS revs into overdrive during panic, initiating the various symptoms of an attack. To manage panic attacks, it can be helpful to understand what is happening inside your body and why.

## HOW PANIC AFFECTS THE BODY

Every symptom of panic you experience is your body's attempt to protect you from a threat. Your heart races faster and pounds harder to send more oxygen more quickly to your muscles. Your blood flow is redirected to large muscles that would be more useful while under attack, such as your thighs. You may feel clamminess or tingling in your extremities because of that redirection of blood.

You don't need to be digesting during a crisis, so energy is also shifted away from the digestive system, which can cause nausea, diarrhea, or dry mouth.

When in danger, we need more oxygen to fuel those large muscles, so we breathe faster and deeper to try to increase that fuel. This can lead to an imbalance in your breathing, which can cause harmless but uncomfortable symptoms such as shortness of breath or chest tightness.

So that you can spring into action, the muscles in your body tense up. That tension can cause body aches, trembling, and trouble relaxing.

You may experience a quick flash of heat and then sweating; these are your body's attempts to prevent you from overheating and make you less easy to grab by an attacker.

## THIS IS YOUR BRAIN ON PANIC

The amygdala, made up of clusters of neurons, is the part of the brain responsible for monitoring your body and your environment for anything that might be dangerous. When it spots a threat, it sends out an alert that leads to the release of adrenaline and cortisol. This sets off your fight-or-flight response—your sense of panic.

When you are in a state of panic, your mind shifts into threat detection, focusing more on possible negatives and worst-case scenarios. Due to breathing imbalances and redirection of blood flow, the supply of blood to your head may be lowered, which can cause uncomfortable but harmless symptoms such as confusion, dizziness, and derealization.

Your amygdala is also constantly learning, attaching emotional importance to situations or objects and creating emotional memories. If you experience fear in a situation, your amygdala stores that information. If you experience the same situation, it brings up that memory of fear again to protect you. This is how panic disorder can begin to develop, a learned fear of fear. If you are experiencing panic disorder, your brain is misinterpreting these internal sensations as signs of danger. The symptoms of panic can be uncomfortable, but none of them are actually dangerous.

*Panic is a sign my body is trying to protect me. Panic is natural and is not here to harm me.*

## Key Takeaways

This chapter helped you understand the roots of panic, including what panic is, where it comes from, and what causes panic attacks. It also reviewed what panic disorder is and how it develops. What's more, you've learned how panic disorder is different from other issues that can lead to panic attacks as well as how panic affects your brain and your body. Here are the takeaways to keep in mind:

- Panic is natural. The changes that happen in your body and brain during a panic attack are occurring to protect you.

- Panic attacks can cause a wide variety of symptoms. They can lead to unintended symptoms that are uncomfortable but harmless in the short term. Panic disorder occurs when your brain misinterprets these internal sensations as signs of danger.

- Becoming aware of your unique symptoms is an important step in panic attack management. Understanding the how and why of your symptoms can help you shift from feeling like a victim to an objective observer.

- You may have inherited a higher sensitivity to panic, but other factors can cause and influence panic, such as major life stressors, specific experiences that evoked fear, anticipatory anxiety, and your beliefs.

- Your amygdala is constantly learning, attaching emotions like fear to memories. Panic disorder can develop due to a learned fear of fear itself.

- If you spend a lot of time worrying about having a panic attack or panic is changing your behaviors in a significant way, you may be suffering from panic disorder. Feeling like panic is taking over your life is a sign to seek professional help.

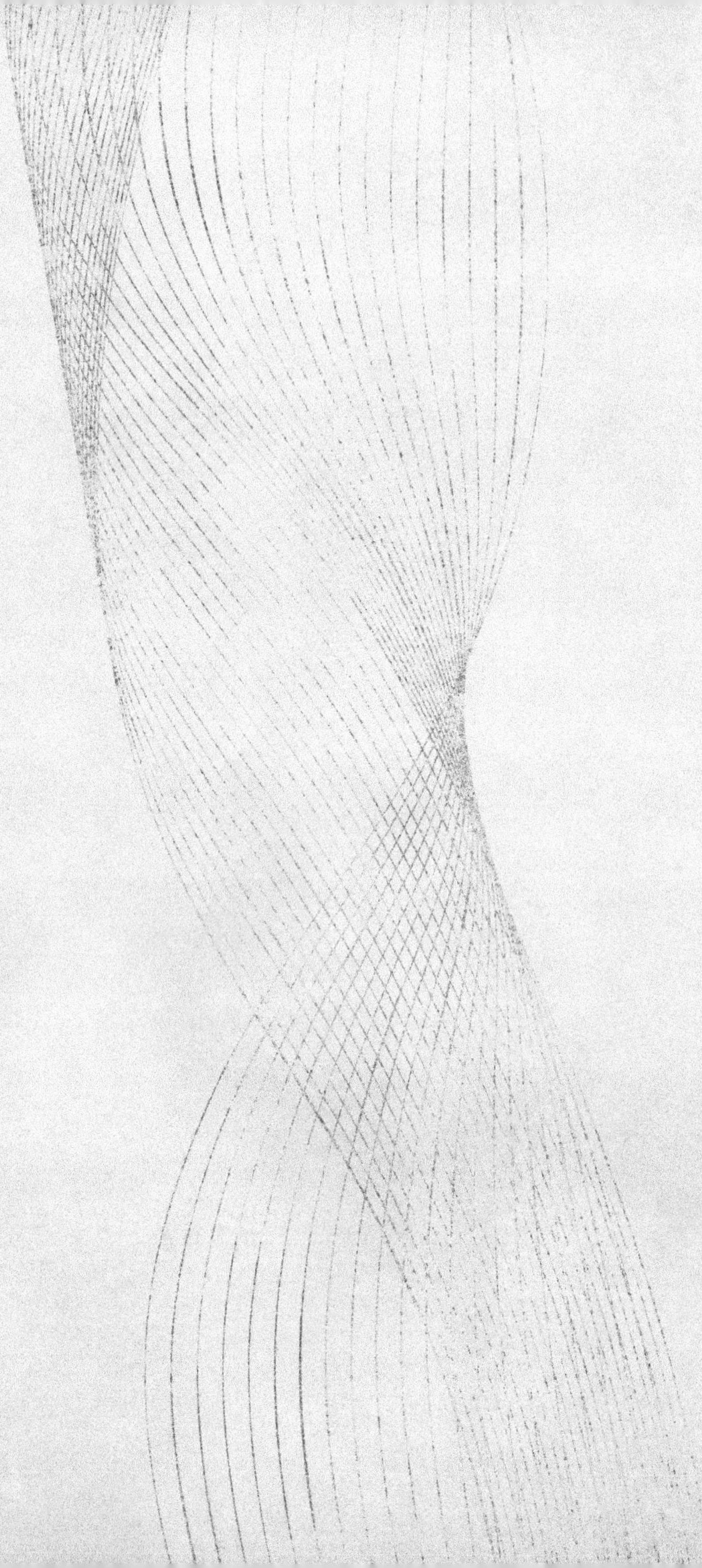

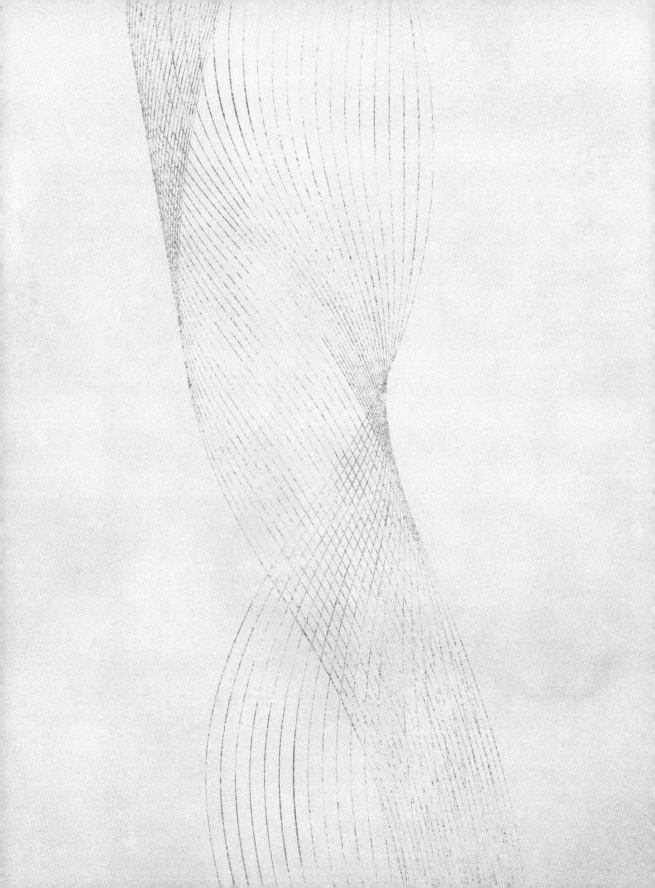

# CHAPTER TWO

# How Is Panic Treated?

You are not doomed to struggle with panic attacks for the rest of your life. Relief is possible. The mental health field can't pinpoint one specific cause for panic, but we've developed techniques for managing many of its most common factors.

Several evidence-based treatments show great success in alleviating panic disorder, including cognitive behavioral therapy (CBT), acceptance and commitment therapy (ACT), and exposure therapy. Medication can be helpful in alleviating intense symptoms of panic. If necessary, short-term medications like benzodiazepines can make the symptoms of panic more manageable. Other medications, such as selective serotonin reuptake inhibitors (SSRIs) and serotonin-norepinephrine reuptake inhibitors (SNRIs), have been shown to be effective in long-term management of panic.

Widespread research has also shown us that panic can be alleviated outside of therapy through mindfulness practices and lifestyle changes, such as a good sleep routine and exercise. Remember, anxiety disorders of all kinds can be treated, and even frequent panic attacks can be managed. This chapter will help you figure out what's best for *you*.

*I don't have to tackle panic alone.*
*There is help out there for me.*

Leanne questioned if nursing was for her. She loved helping people and found the science fascinating, but she didn't know how much longer she could take this recurring feeling during shifts. One look from her senior colleagues, and she was all thumbs, dropping needles and fumbling answers to basic questions.

When she just thought about work, her heart sped up and she started to sweat. She woke up hours before a shift, drilling herself over medications so she wouldn't be caught unprepared. She hated her shifts in the ICU because it was almost impossible to make it to a bathroom if she started to feel panicky. She dreaded the thought that any of her coworkers would notice her anxiety. She feared they would think she was incompetent. If she really was meant for this field, she wouldn't go clammy all over in a patient's room or worry that her supervisor would notice her shaking hands.

It wasn't until Leanne finally got into a therapist's office that she understood what was going on. She hadn't known she was having panic attacks because she was still functioning, still doing her job, and mostly succeeding at hiding it from others. But when her therapist asked if she'd been changing her life in response to her physical symptoms, she began to understand all the ways she had been avoiding panic: over-preparing, dashing to the bathroom if symptoms came on, and carrying a water bottle to prevent even the hint of nausea. She had been living in fear of her panic.

# How Are Panic Attacks Treated?

Panic disorder can be treated through psychotherapy, medication, or a combination of both. As mentioned, common treatments for panic disorder include CBT, ACT, and exposure therapy. Each of these treatments has been researched and found to be effective in reducing symptoms of panic or anxiety.

You can do several things to reduce your panic attacks, even without the help of a health-care professional. Developing a regular mindfulness practice has been shown to reduce anxiety and blood pressure and improve immune function. Making changes to your lifestyle can also help you manage panic, including reducing triggers that overexcite your nervous system, such as caffeine, and engaging in activities that lower your nervous system activation, such as exercise. Let's review your treatment options so you can decide what seems right for you.

# Therapeutic Treatment Options

It is absolutely okay if you need the help of a psychotherapist to address your panic. If you were suffering from a skin condition, you would see a dermatologist. If you are struggling with anxiety or panic that you haven't been able to manage on your own, a psychotherapist can help you.

Cognitive behavioral therapy (CBT) has received the most amount of research and is widely seen as the gold standard of treatment for anxiety disorders. CBT focuses on the connection between your thoughts, feelings, and behaviors. Acceptance and commitment therapy (ACT) incorporates mindfulness to help people accept their thoughts and feelings without judgment and choose to act in line with their values. Exposure therapy is another evidence-based treatment regularly used with panic that involves deliberately confronting the situations that provoke anxiety or panic, with the goal of decreasing the anxiety response and sensitivity over time.

Anxiety disorders respond well to various types of treatment. Despite this, according to the Anxiety and Depression Association of America, only about one-third of people who report struggling with an anxiety disorder seek out treatment. Learning about the different treatment methods can help you find a good fit.

### COGNITIVE BEHAVIORAL THERAPY (CBT)

CBT focuses on helping you understand how your thoughts, feelings, and behaviors influence each other. Often, panic is triggered or exacerbated by your thoughts about the situation, such as "I'm having a heart attack" or "I am going to faint." A CBT-trained therapist will teach you to identify distorted thoughts and challenge them. The goal of CBT is to help you learn to reframe distorted thoughts with more balanced, realistic ones to better regulate your emotions. Over time, you learn to change the thinking patterns and behaviors that were keeping you stuck in the cycle of panic.

## ACCEPTANCE AND COMMITMENT THERAPY (ACT)

ACT has been shown to be effective in the treatment of depression and anxiety disorders. Research has demonstrated it can reduce the severity of panic symptoms. ACT involves cultivating six core skills: (1) acceptance, (2) defusion (detaching from thoughts and feelings), (3) contact with the present moment, (4) self as context, (5) values, and (6) committed action.

The goal of ACT is to help people be more flexible in how they experience and approach life. ACT helps people develop skills to accept their experience mindfully and nonjudgmentally instead of resisting against uncomfortable thoughts and feelings. This acceptance is meant to help them make values-based changes in their lives so they no longer get stuck in their struggles.

## EXPOSURE THERAPY

Exposure therapy has been shown to be highly effective in the treatment of panic disorder. Psychology is a constantly changing field. As the research evolves, we develop a better understanding of how and why exposure therapy works. Per a review of various studies published in 2014 in *Behaviour Research and Therapy*, research points to habituation, fear extinction, and inhibitory learning as factors involved in exposure therapy.

Habituation is the process in which the nervous system gets used to stimuli through repeated, prolonged contact. An example of habituation is when you jump into a cold pool. It's freezing at first, until you habituate to the sensation. Inhibitory learning is the process in which, through experience, you develop new associations with your trigger that can inhibit your old fear association. This treatment works by exposing the person to the feared object or situation to extinguish the fear response over time.

Exposure therapy usually involves identifying a list of a person's fears and then exposing them to those fears, either gradually or intensely all at once. Keep in mind, exposure therapy is designed for fears that are not actually harmful. Your fear response is necessary to protect you from real danger. If you experience panic disorder, you fear the sensations of panic themselves. Exposure would involve creating a list of sensations you fear and systematically re-creating those sensations, such as spinning around to spur the feeling of dizziness.

If you are dealing with panic disorder with agoraphobia specifically, you also fear specific situations where you feel like you can't get away. Your therapist would help you create a list of situations and factors related to them, such as going to a party with or without the ability to drive yourself home, and help you deliberately expose yourself to those.

# Treating Panic with Mindfulness

When you are panicking, you are hyperfixated on your body's responses. Your thoughts are racing, spiraling into the scariest worst-case scenarios. Mindfulness can be an antidote to anxiety and panic. Mindfulness is nonjudgmental awareness of the present moment. It is developed through the practice of focusing on something in the present, often on the breath, to learn to regulate what your mind pays attention to.

Practicing mindfulness is essentially strengthening your ability to be aware, to shift your attention at will without judging the experience. Awareness of what's happening inside your body and mind can help you change your responses to it. You can learn to spot thoughts that are spiraling out of control. You can actively notice what's going on in your body and respond in a more productive way. For instance, if you are feeling panicked, being mindful would involve accepting and acknowledging that fact in the moment, without judging or trying to change it.

Resistance is often what makes our emotional experience more difficult. When you practice mindfulness, you are not trying to be or do anything besides maintaining moment-to-moment awareness. You notice all the various sensations that come up, including physical feelings, emotions, and thoughts. Becoming distracted is a normal part of the process. The aim is to notice distraction and then bring your attention back to the present moment. Being able to observe and accept your experience is a key skill in panic attack management.

# Additional Treatment Options

There are several other things you can do to help you manage your panic. Medication can be effective in reducing the symptoms of a panic attack. Common medications for panic include selective serotonin reuptake inhibitors (SSRIs), serotonin-norepinephrine reuptake inhibitors (SNRIs), and benzodiazepines. Lifestyle changes can also help you better cope with panic, including a good sleep routine, relaxation activities, exercise, and reducing triggers that overstimulate your nervous system.

### MEDICATION

SSRIs and SNRIs, types of antidepressants, are some of the most commonly prescribed medications for panic disorder. They carry a low risk of serious side effects and are effective long term. They have also been shown to assist with the process of exposure through promoting growth and change in neurons.

Benzodiazepines cause a calming effect on the amygdala, reducing symptoms of anxiety. They are effective in the short term but are not recommended for long-term use as they are habit-forming. Benzodiazepines have also been shown to decrease the effectiveness of exposure therapy due to reducing the activation of the amygdala. Every person has a unique response to psychiatric medication, so if you are interested in exploring medication, consult with a doctor to determine what's right for you.

## LIFESTYLE CHANGES

Small changes in your life can help make anxiety and panic more manageable. Exercise has been shown to reduce the activation of your SNS (the gas pedal that flares up your panic symptoms). Exercise causes many of the same symptoms associated with a panic attack, such as sweating or a racing heart. Research, such as that published in *Anxiety, Stress, & Coping* in 2008, has shown that exercise can also act like exposure therapy, reducing a person's discomfort with those symptoms.

Improving your sleep routine can help reduce your panic. There is evidence that lack of sleep causes difficulty concentrating and memory issues and worsens mood, which can contribute to panic.

Activation of your PNS (the brake) calms your body to bring it back to its resting state. Relaxation activities can be used to activate your PNS, manually telling your body to calm down. These include activities such as deep breathing and muscle relaxation. These activities can be helpful if they are used to support you in confronting your panic instead of avoiding it.

Certain things increase the activation of your SNS, such as caffeine, stress, and some medications. Learning to identify your triggers can help you reduce your general level of anxiety and thus reduce your chances of experiencing panic.

## Seeking Guidance from a Medical Professional

As you've been learning, panic is made up of several different components: your thoughts, behaviors, physical sensations, and unique triggers. That can be a lot to navigate on your own. Understanding what is causing your panic and developing an effective plan to treat it can be difficult without help. This workbook can help you learn tools to cope with panic, but it cannot take the place of a health-care professional.

If you feel panic is affecting many different areas of your life or keeping you from pursuing your goals, contact a health-care provider. I encourage you to specifically seek out a psychotherapist who specializes in anxiety. It's best to work with someone who has studied the research and evidence-based interventions in depth to make sure they understand all aspects of your problems and the best way to help you.

In general, the earlier you get professional help, the better the outcome. If you are going back and forth in your head about whether therapy is for you, just pick up the phone or send that email to connect with a possible provider. They'll be able to help you determine if you need mental health treatment or provide you helpful resources.

To find a psychotherapist, you can contact your insurance for a list of in-network providers. You can also search various online databases. There are even databases where you can seek out therapists with a specific background. Suggestions for these databases can be found in the Resources on page 184. You can also ask the people around you for recommendations.

*Asking for help when I need it is*
*a sign of awareness and strength.*

## Key Takeaways

In this chapter, you learned that panic can be treated in various ways, including with psychotherapy and medication. This chapter also reviewed the many things you can do in your everyday life to manage panic. Here are this chapter's key takeaways:

- Relief is possible. Panic disorder can be managed in various ways. Anxiety disorders respond well to treatment. Three specific types of treatment that have been shown to be effective are CBT, ACT, and exposure therapy. Medications can be used to either alleviate short-term symptoms or help you manage panic in the long term.

- Mindfulness has been shown to reduce anxiety and increase self-awareness. Cultivating awareness can help you better cope with panic by helping you reduce judgment of your experience, identify your triggers, and respond in a healthier way.

- Several changes you can make in your life can help reduce panic. Exercise, relaxation activities, and getting enough sleep help reduce your general level of stress. Learning about triggers that excite your nervous system can help you manage them better.

- If you plan to seek out therapy, find a psychotherapist who specializes in anxiety so you can be sure they understand the science of panic and the most effective interventions to help you.

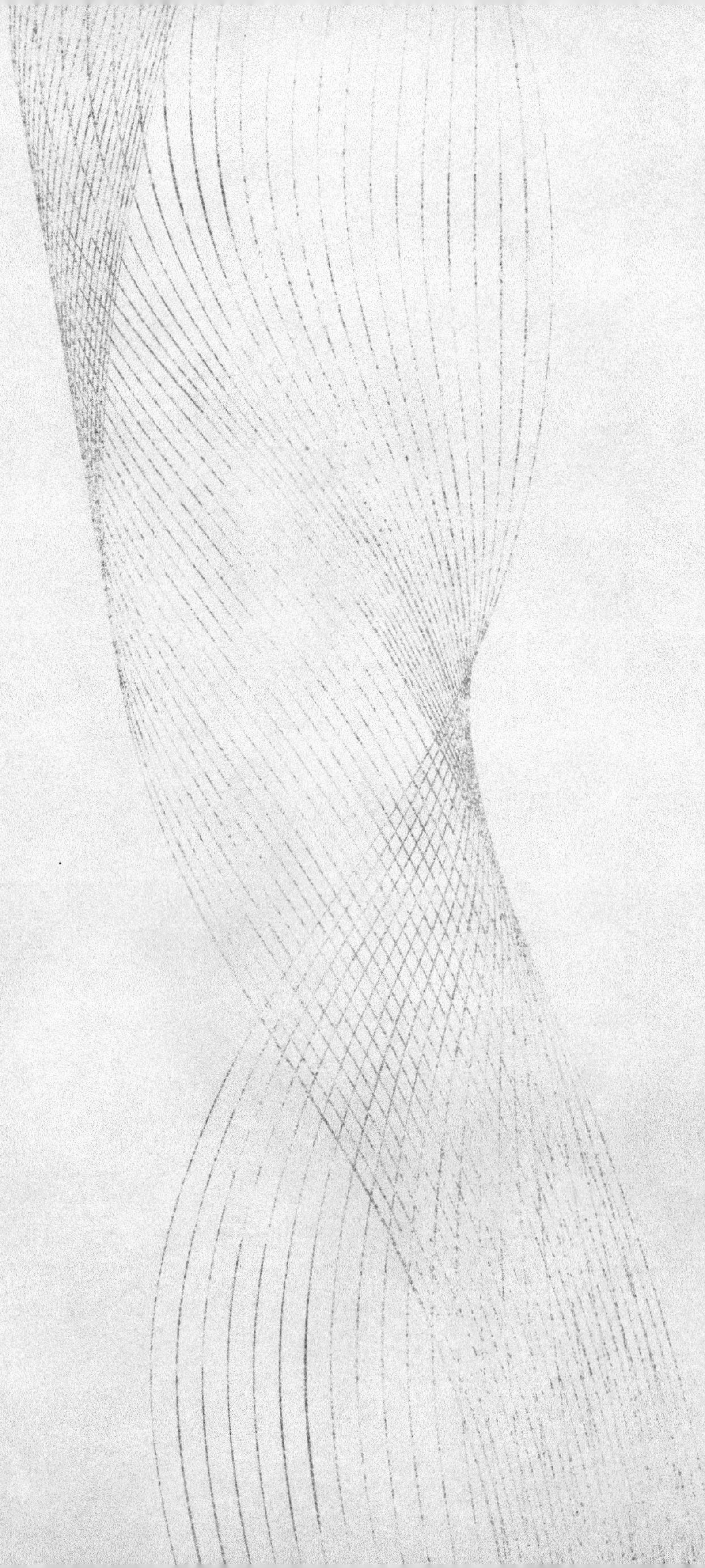

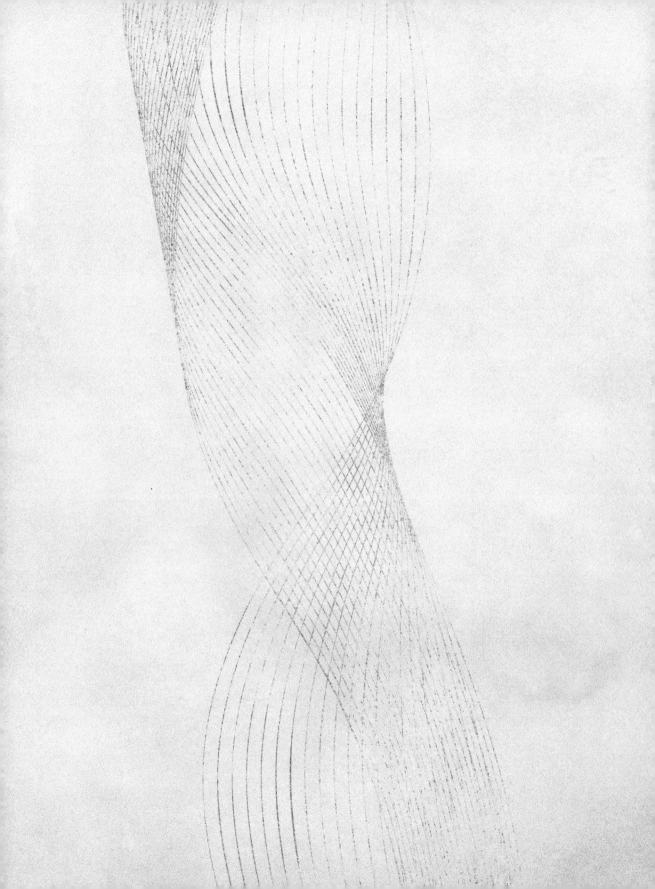

# CHAPTER THREE

# Your Panic Attack Relief Plan

Panic is a very personal experience. You've been learning about the many factors that trigger or influence it. Now it's time to learn how you can manage it for yourself. This chapter reviews the seven-week plan you will use to learn about your cycle of panic. What causes it? What reduces it? How can you manage it in the long term? You will learn the specifics behind each step before you get started.

Because panic can take so many different forms and be affected by so many things, this chapter stresses the importance of a uniquely tailored plan for effective panic attack management. It also teaches you the importance of tracking your symptoms so that you get a complete understanding of your panic. By chapter's end, you will have a good understanding of what you need to implement in your plan.

*Relief is possible. To overcome my panic, I need to learn what works for me.*

Samara sat in her car, staring at the wheel. She had her journal with her in the passenger seat and her phone in case she got lost. She knew she would be fine. She told herself this, but it didn't stop her throat from feeling like it was closing up. Her chest ached, but she reminded herself that she was definitely not having a heart attack. Her recent EKG proved her heart was pounding along like it should.

As she was about to face one of her biggest triggers, Samara's mind was shouting at her to run away. Samara had been working with her therapist for weeks now, identifying how she experienced panic in her body, what her triggers were, and tools she could use in the moment. She knew this was normal and that these sensations were a sign of her panic because she was afraid of driving. Through therapy, she had learned how having a panic attack while driving had affected her nervous system, setting it up to get triggered anytime she was reminded of the experience.

Samara had also gotten very clear on her goals. She was sick of feeling trapped in her apartment because she wouldn't touch her car. So, she was going to face it. She repeated the statement she had practiced with her therapist aloud: "This feeling is not going to hurt me. I need to face this feeling so my brain can learn that driving isn't a scary thing." Samara turned the ignition key, feeling afraid but finally ready to stop letting that fear control her.

# Panic Attack Management Looks Different for Everyone

Panic attacks can only be managed if you understand your unique triggers, your life experiences that have led you to panic, and the tools that work for you to confront your fears. No two panic attacks look exactly alike, even for the same person. That also means that panic attack management is constantly shifting. What may have worked for you in one moment might be completely useless in the next. That doesn't mean it's not possible to manage your panic. It does mean you have to put in the work to learn about yourself and develop an effective strategy.

The things that trigger you might be completely benign to other people. And that's okay. Your triggers have been developed from your personal experiences. They aren't a sign of weakness or cowardice. They are simply the result of how your unique body and mind have interacted with the world. Maybe you're afraid of fast-food restaurants because that's the first place you had a panic attack. Maybe you can't take your children to a theme park because the crowds terrify you. Maybe you hate deep breathing because you fixate on how you think you're doing it wrong. Learning to manage your panic with the help of this workbook is a matter of discovering what works for you and reminding yourself there is *nothing* wrong with you.

## How the Seven-Week Plan Can Help

This plan will not eliminate your panic entirely. In fact, nothing will get rid of your panic or anxiety altogether, but that isn't the goal. Remember, you need your anxiety and panic in situations where there is a real threat. It has a purpose. So, we aren't aiming to get rid of your panic.

Instead, you will learn how to read your cycle of anxiety and panic so you can get relief from your overwhelming symptoms. Responding to your panic in a different way can lower the intensity and frequency of your symptoms so panic no longer gets in the way of your life. This requires you to develop tools for long-term and short-term situations. It's the beginning of a lifestyle change. In seven weeks, you will have learned how to have a healthy relationship with your panic and what you need to do for the rest of your life to keep that relationship healthy.

This plan is structured to give you relief quickly if you actively practice the things you learn. After the seven weeks, it will be up to you to continue implementing them. If you find yourself struggling and in need of professional help, you can work on this plan with a health-care provider, too.

### WEEK ONE
#### *UNDERSTAND HOW PANIC IMPACTS YOUR WELL-BEING*
To understand how to address panic, you must first understand how it affects you. In week one, you will learn to identify your symptoms of panic and the mental health issues that might be relevant to you. You will learn your triggers for panic and how panic affects different areas of your life. You will also learn helpful tools you can use along the way, including skills to cultivate awareness of your mind and body and techniques to break the hold panic has on you in the moment.

## WEEK TWO
### DETERMINE YOUR NEEDS AND GOALS

In week two, activities will guide you to identify your specific needs around panic and your goals in the short and long term. You'll review how to apply wellness practices such as exercise and good sleep hygiene to your own life to address your needs and goals. This will then help you identify other factors that affect your panic so you can develop strategies to address them. You will also explore the things you value to leverage your motivation for change.

## WEEK THREE
### IDENTIFY WHERE YOU STRUGGLE

In week three, you will identify your barriers to addressing panic, behaviors keeping you stuck in the cycle, and the roots of some of your fears. Along the way, you will continue to learn tools to help you cope with your struggles, including activities to help you keep yourself accountable as you stick to the plan. You will explore what hasn't worked for you and why, so you can use that knowledge to help you succeed.

## WEEK FOUR
### BREAK THE CYCLE OF NEGATIVE THOUGHTS

In week four, you will learn how your thoughts contribute to your cycle of panic and uncover tools to interrupt that cycle. What kinds of thoughts do you experience related to your panic? How do they affect you? This week, you will learn to spot distorted thoughts that lead your nervous system to overreact. You will practice effective strategies to reframe those thoughts and respond in a healthier way. Over time, using these skills can reduce your panic in the moment and shift your perspective to a more helpful and balanced one for the future.

## WEEK FIVE
### FACING YOUR FEARS

By week five, you will be ready to confront your fears and learn how exposure therapy can help you overcome your panic. This week, you will create and implement an exposure plan for yourself. You will gradually face your fears to take back control of your life. You will also explore and track how exposure changes your beliefs about your triggers and yourself.

## WEEK SIX
### *EMBRACING THE MOMENT WITH*
### *MINDFULNESS AND MEDITATION*

Week six will focus on mindfulness and meditation. You will learn more about the benefits of meditation and how to practice it, including basic mindfulness meditations, loving-kindness meditations, and ways to practice mindfulness in your daily activities. This week, you will explore your past beliefs about and experiences with meditation and learn tips to address any possible struggles. You will discover what kind of practice suits you best and how to incorporate it into your panic attack management plan.

## WEEK SEVEN
### *BRINGING ALL THE PIECES TOGETHER*

The last week of your plan will review everything you've learned. You will recall your original goals and review your progress toward those goals. You will identify the tools that worked best for you so you can make sure to consistently come back to them. You will celebrate your accomplishments and identify areas of continued struggle. You will explore how to troubleshoot those struggles and where to go for help when you need it. You will work on how to sustain and build on your progress for the future.

## The Importance of Symptom Tracking

Tracking your experience is essential to your panic attack management plan. Remember, the only way to overcome your panic is to get a clear understanding of your unique experience of it. Regularly tracking your symptoms will help you accomplish that. I recommend getting a notebook specifically for your panic attack plan so you can keep all the things you've learned in an easily accessible and organized place.

Here's how symptom tracking supports you and your plan. First, awareness of any problem helps you better understand how to address the issue. Consistently tracking your symptoms will help you learn how panic attacks affect you in detail, including how it affects your body, thoughts, and behaviors. Tracking your symptoms will also help you understand what factors trigger your panic, such as specific situations, and the factors that help alleviate your panic, such as strategies you've found to be effective.

Panic often makes people feel out of control. A greater awareness of your panic through tracking will give you a sense of control because it will no longer feel like a mystery. Being consistent about your tracking will ensure that you have a precise record of your panic; you won't have to rely on your memory, which is much less accurate. Having an accurate record will also help you track your progress. Instead of a general overview of how you're doing, you will be able to see the actual changes happening over time so you can keep practicing what works for you and let go of things that don't.

# What You'll Need to Get Started

To face the overwhelming feeling of panic, you will need to be compassionate toward yourself. This plan will ask you to directly engage with your struggle. You'll need to navigate some things that will make you uncomfortable or seem counterintuitive. Keep an open mind and hold off on judgments of the specific activities until you've had a chance to practice them. You don't need harsh criticism in facing your panic. You will need kindness and understanding to confront your fears.

As you start to work your way through this plan, it's important to lean on your support system. Get clear on who you can include in your panic attack plan so you can remember you're not alone when you find yourself struggling.

For this plan to be effective, you will need to dedicate a few hours per week, keep yourself accountable, and be willing to be vulnerable. There are also several resources that will be helpful, including apps to support your use of healthy coping tools and further learning from outside sources.

Let's take a closer look now at each of the qualities that will lead you toward success.

## AN OPEN MIND

Think of panic like an ocean. In the ocean, you must swim directly forward and under the waves to get past them. You'll never outrun the ocean no matter how hard you try; you have to engage with it head-on and let it pass. Many of the activities you will be asked to do in the next seven weeks will feel dangerous, like you're running straight into your fear. Keep an open mind and remember that treating panic can feel counterintuitive, but the science shows us these tools can work.

## SELF-COMPASSION

When you witness someone's suffering, compassion is the shared sense of that suffering and motivation to alleviate that person's hurt. Self-compassion is directing that same supportive response to yourself when you are struggling. Self-compassion has been shown in various studies to increase positive mood, motivation, healthy behaviors, and resilience. Practicing self-compassion makes it easier for you to get up and try again when you struggle and to admit your mistakes so you can grow from them. Believe it or not, self-compassion can actually be learned even if you don't have much practice, and several of the activities will show you how.

## A SUPPORT SYSTEM

There are times when all this will be hard. Talk to the people you trust before you start the plan and ask for help. You will need support to get through it, including the cooperation of those closest to you to help you change some of your unhelpful patterns. Working through this plan may actually open your social world, making it easier for you to build closer relationships.

## ACCOUNTABILITY

You will need to be accountable to yourself to succeed with your plan. This means setting aside a few hours per week to honestly engage with this workbook and with yourself, even when it's scary. There are many tools at your disposal to help you do this, like apps, books, and podcasts (see the Resources on page 184).

*With commitment, honesty, and support, it is possible to stop panic from controlling my life.*

# Key Takeaways

This chapter showed you the different aspects of your seven-week plan for panic attack management. Throughout it, you learned about what you will need to implement this plan and the different areas of your panic that it will target. Keep these main takeaways in mind:

- Learning to manage your panic must be tailored to your unique experience. To address your panic, you will have to identify your personal triggers, life experiences that contribute to your panic, and a diverse set of tools that work for you.

- The goal of this seven-week plan is not to eliminate your panic. The goal of this plan is to help you manage your panic in a healthy way and get relief from your overwhelming symptoms. You will learn about your cycle of anxiety and panic and acquire tools you can use to manage your panic in the short and long term.

- For this plan to be successful, you need to dedicate time to practice the skills, be compassionate with yourself, and have an open mind. You will also need to be ready to be honest and keep yourself accountable.

- Having support is an important aspect of this plan. Identify and use the social supports available to you. There are also outside resources you can turn to for additional support.

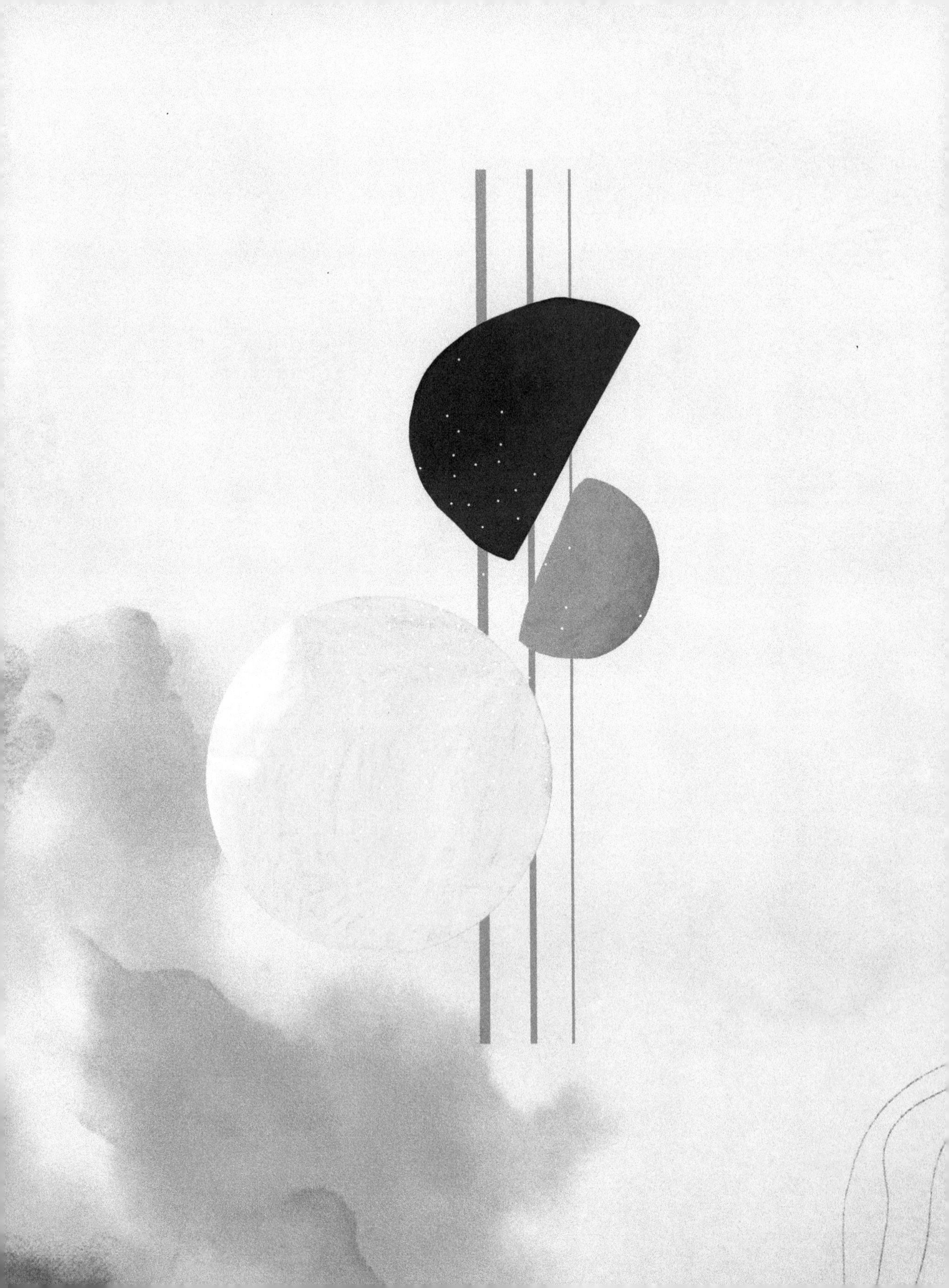

# PART TWO

# YOUR SEVEN-WEEK PLAN

You are now ready to get started with your seven-week plan. Each week, you will be engaging in activities in this workbook, plus learning practices you can turn to in your everyday life. Through a combination of prompts, exercises, and affirmations, you will gain insight into your personal experience of panic and discover practical tools to manage it.

Complete the activities and exercises in order, as many of them build on each other. You may complete some sections faster than within a week, or you may need to take longer. However, be sure to follow the instructions for any activities that are meant to be done more than once, such as monitoring your symptoms daily.

The first three weeks of your plan will focus on developing your understanding of your panic. From there, you will learn how thoughts can worsen panic. You will explore the thoughts related to your panic and how to shift your thinking from unhelpful thought patterns to a more realistic and helpful way of responding.

You will learn and practice effective tools throughout the weeks to help you cope with your panic. Using those tools to support you, you will then develop a plan to confront what has been keeping you stuck in your cycle of panic. Throughout this plan, you will learn the benefits of mindfulness and develop a practice of your own. Continue to use the tools you learn from week to week, building a routine that allows you to manage panic during week eight and beyond.

*I do not have to feel this way forever. A panic attack is a temporary experience that will pass.*

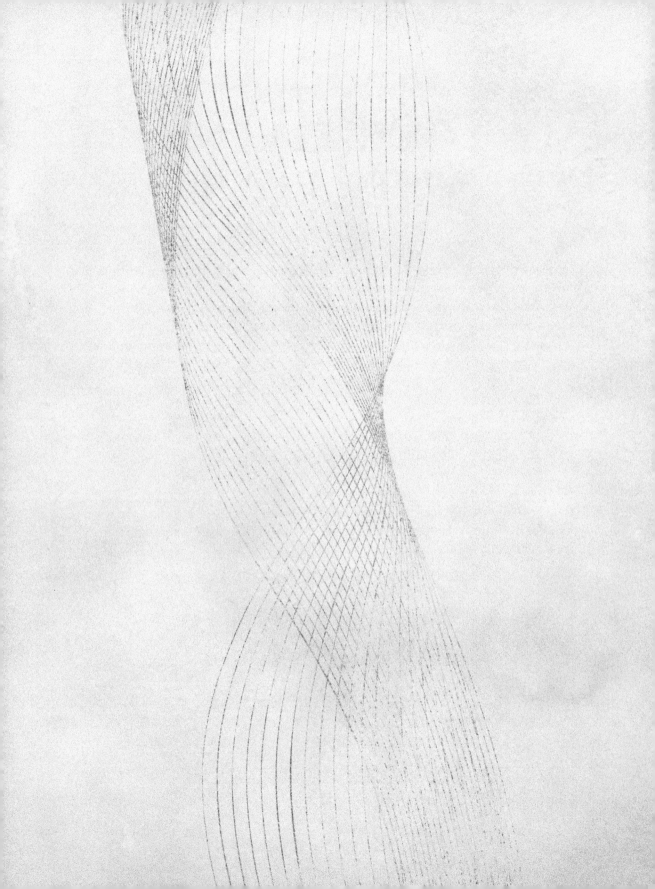

# Understand How Panic Impacts Your Well-Being

It's time to explore the many ways panic has been impacting your life. You will identify your own panic attack symptoms and learn about possible mental health issues you could be struggling with. You will also learn practices to build awareness of your panic as well as tools to ease your symptoms in the short term. You will use these exercises to help prepare you to confront your fears in the future. Exercises this week will help you identify how panic has affected your behaviors, relationships, and activities. To wrap up, you will weigh the pros and cons of facing your panic to help you connect to your motivation and readiness for change.

Liam didn't eat out alone. He would not ask a store employee a question even if he really needed help. He never stayed overnight with friends. Without even realizing it, Liam did everything in his power to feel like he was in control. He drove himself everywhere, made sure he always had an excuse to leave if he needed it, and rarely tried new activities.

Liam thought he was doing all the right things. He thought it made sense to avoid anything that would make him panic. If he didn't let himself think about it and did everything he could to avoid his anxiety, he figured he could manage it.

Liam had his first panic attack about a year ago. The first time, he thought it was a fluke. He had been really stressed over some work deadlines and was getting very little sleep trying to get his reports in on time. He had always felt like an anxious person, so he wasn't surprised that so much stress triggered a panic attack. What was surprising and confusing was that the attacks continued. They began to get worse, happening more often.

To prevent any possibility of panic, Liam started to make small changes. They brought relief in the moment, making him feel like he was on the right track. The thing was, he had recently started noticing that the list of things he could do was getting smaller and smaller. He found he was having to avoid more and more things, and his panic attacks weren't going away.

# How Is Panic Controlling Your Life?

Dealing with panic is not just about your experience of it in the moment. When panic attacks strike, they are incredibly disruptive. Panic interrupts whatever it was you were doing at that time, stealing away your focus and probably impacting your mood for a while afterward. But that is not the only way panic affects you. Because panic is such a horrible feeling, many people who struggle with panic attacks start to change the way they are living their lives to avoid future attacks. Panic can affect the activities you engage in, your behaviors, and your relationships.

Learning about how panic affects your life is the first step toward learning how to manage it. In your attempts to get away from panic, you've likely let it start to control you. It can feel like a vise, slowly constricting your life more and more. Identifying the different areas panic influences in your life will help you learn what you need to address.

# PANIC ATTACK SYMPTOMS CHECKLIST

As a reminder, a panic attack is defined as an intense surge of fear, paired with four or more physiological symptoms of panic. To better understand your panic, check off any symptoms you've experienced. The last four symptoms are not part of the formal criteria for panic attacks but are often associated with them.

- ☐ Heart pounding or racing
- ☐ Sweating, trembling, or shaking
- ☐ Shortness of breath or the feeling of being smothered
- ☐ Feeling of choking
- ☐ Chest pain or discomfort
- ☐ Nausea or upset stomach
- ☐ Feeling dizzy, unsteady, lightheaded, or faint
- ☐ Hot or cold flashes
- ☐ Paresthesia (numbness or tingling, especially in the hands or feet)

- ☐ Derealization (feeling "off," surreal, things seeming noticeably distorted)
- ☐ Depersonalization (feeling detached from yourself, including an out-of-body experience)
- ☐ Thinking you are losing control
- ☐ Thinking you are dying
- ☐ Thinking you are going crazy
- ☐ Frequent urination
- ☐ Dry mouth
- ☐ Blurred vision or spots in your vision
- ☐ Vomiting or diarrhea

Take a moment to think about times in the past when you've experienced four or more of these symptoms at once. Describe your memories:

_____

_____

_____

# BODY SCAN PRACTICE

A body scan is a type of meditation that involves slowly and systematically paying attention to different parts of your body to notice any sensations that may be coming up. The goal of a body scan is not to change these sensations, but to become more connected to your physical experience in a mindful, nonjudgmental way.

To practice, read along with this script or listen back to a recording. Body scans can also be found on meditation apps if you'd prefer to listen along to someone else. Do this practice once a day for about five to ten minutes.

1. Find a comfortable position. Take a few deep breaths to allow yourself to slow down.

2. Now bring your attention to your feet. Notice any sensations there, any tingling or tightness.

3. Slowly move your attention to your legs, noticing any pressure or pain along your calves, knees, or thighs. Notice these sensations without judgment and without trying to change anything.

4. Now move your attention to your torso. Notice any tension or pain from your abdomen to your back to your chest. Notice any pleasant sensations. Simply observe anything that is coming up.

5. When you are ready, focus on your arms and shoulders, paying attention to any discomfort or pleasure. You might not feel anything. Notice that.

6. Shift your attention to your head, moving your focus along your cheeks, nose, forehead, all the way up to your scalp. Observe any sensations occurring there.

7. Bring your attention back to the room. Start to slowly move your body, and open your eyes when you are ready.

# LABEL YOUR EMOTIONS

Panic is one of many emotions. And several emotions may affect your sense of panic. You might start your day feeling frustrated because you couldn't find your keys, then feel embarrassed because you showed up late to work, and then become anxious at the thought of your boss finding out—and all of that could contribute to becoming panicked. Panic attack management is about more than just panic itself. To cope with panic in a healthy way, it is important for you to be able to understand and regulate *all* your emotions.

An emotion is a temporary, subjective state of being, usually described in one word, and usually involving some physical sensation. An emotions wheel like the one that follows can help you put a more specific label on what you are feeling. For each emotion you label, notice any physical sensations you are experiencing. Do this daily.

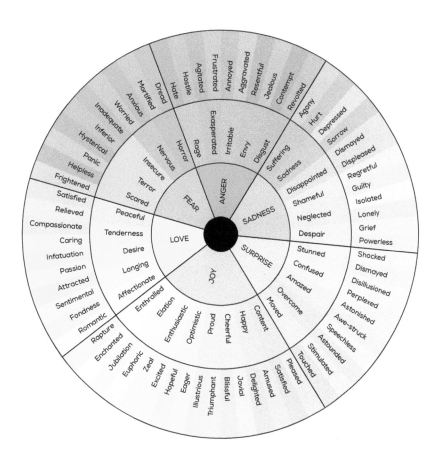

# RECOGNIZE YOUR PANIC ATTACKS

Now that you have been practicing identifying your emotions and physical sensations, you have a better awareness of your panic. To stop your panic from spiraling, it is important to recognize it in the moment. The next time you realize you are having a panic attack, try this:

1. Consciously recognize the panic attack. Avoidance reinforces fear because it teaches your body that the thing you avoid is something to be afraid of. So, instead of distracting yourself or ignoring your panic attack, label it for what it is.

2. Remind yourself that all emotions are temporary, and panic will pass. Remember, although panic is uncomfortable, it will not hurt you in the short term.

3. Identify the physical sensations you are feeling in the moment. Recognize that this feeling is stemming from your body's natural response to fear. Most panic attacks last fewer than twenty minutes. If there is no real threat, tell yourself that you are not in danger and just need to ride out the experience until it inevitably ends.

# KEEP A PANIC ATTACK LOG

Maintaining a log of your panic attacks will help you better understand them. This week, start keeping track of where the attack happened, details about the situation, any emotions you might be feeling, and any physical sensations you experienced. Here's an example:

## SAMPLE PANIC ATTACK LOG

| Date/Time | Situation | Emotions | Sensations |
|---|---|---|---|
| *Tuesday, April 10th, at 12:00 p.m.* | *Meeting a new person at a coffee shop* | *Panic, anxiety, embarrassment* | *Heart racing, hands shaking, derealization, nausea* |
| *Monday, April 16th, at 8:00 p.m.* | *Having in-laws over for dinner* | *Panic, guilt, shame* | *Hyperventilating, chest pain, heat, shaking* |
| *Saturday, May 1st, at 11:00 a.m.* | *Getting on a plane* | *Panic, terror* | *Trembling, heart pounding, shortness of breath, dizzy* |
| *Wednesday, June 7th, at 6:00 p.m.* | *Being at a concert* | *Panic, embarrassment, anger* | *Heart racing, hands shaking, upset stomach, chest pain* |

Use this log to detail your panic attacks:

## PANIC ATTACK LOG

| Date/Time | Situation | Emotions | Sensations |
|---|---|---|---|
| | | | |
| | | | |
| | | | |
| | | | |

# HOW DOES PANIC AFFECT YOUR LIFE?

Although panic is not harmful in the short term, excessive anxiety or panic over time can wear on the body, possibly causing longer-term problems such as high blood pressure or digestive issues. It can also prevent you from doing the things necessary to live a healthy lifestyle. Panic can also get in the way of your everyday responsibilities, like driving on the freeway or taking your dog for a walk. For more insight, describe how panic affects you in the different areas of your life:

**Relationships:**

_____

_____

_____

**Work/School:**

_____

_____

_____

**Health/Physical:**

_____

_____

_____

**Daily Activities:**

_____

_____

_____

# MENTAL HEALTH DISORDERS QUIZ

Panic attacks can be a symptom of many different mental health disorders. The quiz has six parts; each covers a different mental health issue that can lead to panic. Give yourself one point for every symptom you experience in each category and tally your score for each.

## Agoraphobia

☐ I avoid any situation that I can't escape from easily.

☐ I am always aware of the exits and have a plan to leave if I become anxious.

☐ I fear other people witnessing me having a panic attack.

☐ I am afraid of having unpleasant bodily sensations in public.

Score:_____

## Generalized Anxiety Disorder

☐ I worry about a lot of different things.

☐ I have trouble controlling my worry.

☐ I am so restless I find it hard to sleep or relax.

☐ I feel tense most of the time or often feel aches and pains.

Score:_____

## Obsessive Compulsive Disorder

☐ I have intrusive, repetitive thoughts.

☐ These thoughts cause me a lot of distress.

☐ I have rituals or certain behaviors I do over and over again to help me feel better.

☐ If I cannot do my rituals or behaviors, I feel really bad.

Score:_____

### Post-traumatic Stress Disorder

☐ I have flashbacks, nightmares, or intrusive thoughts or feelings about a traumatic experience.

☐ I avoid things that remind me of my trauma.

☐ I have been feeling very bad or overly sensitive, startling easily, becoming angry quickly, or having lots of negative thoughts.

☐ I am not interested in things I used to enjoy, or I am doing risky/destructive things.

Score:_____

### Social Anxiety Disorder

☐ I worry about how others will perceive me.

☐ I avoid social situations.

☐ I worry I will do something embarrassing or offensive.

☐ I experience anxiety or panic related to social situations, such as public speaking.

Score:_____

### Specific Phobia

☐ I am intensely afraid of a specific thing like heights or needles.

☐ I avoid the thing I am afraid of.

☐ My fear of this specific thing is more extreme than most people's reactions.

☐ I feel anxiety or panic only when I encounter this specific thing.

Score:_____

Notice which areas have the highest scores. Where do most of your symptoms cluster? You can share the results of this quiz with a health-care provider so they can assess you for any possible diagnosis.

# WHAT DO YOU AVOID?

Because panic attacks can be so terrifying and uncomfortable, many people start to plan their lives around their panic. You may stop going to social gatherings, the place you experienced your first panic attack, or anywhere you don't feel you can easily escape, such as a crowded restaurant.

Think about the places or activities you used to enjoy. Are you avoiding any of those places or activities because you are afraid of becoming panicked, having to leave suddenly, or embarrassing yourself? Being as specific as you can about the details, list those things here:

_____

_____

_____

_____

# DEEP BREATHING EXERCISE

When you feel anxiety or panic, you breathe faster and deeper to send more oxygen to your large muscles. This may lead to hyperventilation, also called overbreathing. Hyperventilation happens when you breathe in too rapidly, taking in more oxygen than your body needs. This lowers the levels of carbon dioxide in your blood, causing symptoms such as dizziness, confusion, and chest pain. These symptoms can then feed into your panic, making you more distressed and leading to more overbreathing.

When you understand that overbreathing is exacerbating your panic, then you know what you can do to interrupt the cycle: Focus on slowing and controlling your breathing to bring it back into balance. You will eventually practice facing the sensations of panic and anxiety to help you learn you don't need to be afraid of them, but in the meantime deep breathing is a great tool to help you regulate your breath. The following is a simple but effective breathing technique called box breathing. Be sure not to breathe quickly or too deeply while practicing.

1. Inhale slowly for a count of two.

2. Keep the air in your lungs for a count of two.

CONTINUED ▶

3. Slowly exhale for a count of two.

4. Repeat several times, making sure to focus on the sensation of your breath.

This exercise is not meant to take away your anxiety or panic. Remember, trying to get away from your anxiety or panic is avoidance, and that would only reinforce your fear. Instead, use deep breathing to help you face your anxiety or panic while you are doing the activities and exercises in this workbook.

*I can use deep breathing to face my fears.*

## IDENTIFY THE THREAT

Panic is meant to protect us from a serious threat. You can think of a threat not just as physical harm, but as any negative outcome you fear or strongly want to avoid. Recognizing what you are perceiving as the threat helps you problem-solve for the actual danger. This also helps you challenge any distorted thoughts leading you to believe that something is threatening when it is not.

The following is a list of common fears related to panic. Check off any you have experienced and add any others that come to mind.

☐ People will judge me negatively (for example, they'll think I'm weak/crazy/incompetent/a burden).

☐ I will lose control/go crazy and embarrass or hurt myself.

☐ I cannot handle this feeling.

☐ This feeling will last forever or get worse.

☐ I will have a heart attack.

☐ I will faint.

☐ I will be seriously hurt by "X" (e.g., a dog, driving, flying).

☐ I will lose my job or place in school.

☐ I will lose my relationships.

☐ There is something wrong with me, and it can't be fixed.

☐ My panic will prevent me from being successful or competent.

☐ My panic will make people around me feel unsafe.

☐ Other: _____

☐ Other: _____

# GROUNDING PRACTICE

If you've reached this point in the book, you've been doing a fantastic amount of work to confront your panic. Sometimes, however, the sensations or thoughts you are experiencing can feel too overwhelming if you aren't ready to face them. Grounding is a technique you can use to anchor yourself in the present moment if your distress becomes too intense.

Grounding works by shifting your attention away from the source of your panic to something neutral. It is not a tool that will manage your panic in the long term, but it can allow your body to calm down so you can address your panic without it feeling so overwhelming.

There are countless forms of grounding, and physical grounding is one of the most common. Physical grounding involves moving your focus to any one of your five senses. An easy way to remember how to do this is the 5-4-3-2-1 technique, as follows:

1. Look around the room and describe five things you can see, being as mindful as you can. Pay attention to all the details, including color, shape, or size.

2. Now focus on four things you can feel, noticing things such as temperature, weight, or texture.

3. Then concentrate on three things you can hear.

4. Next, identify two things you can smell, even the absence of smell.

5. Last, focus on one thing you can taste.

Remember, you are not trying to feed into the idea that anxiety or panic is dangerous, but you also don't want to stop doing these activities if you become overwhelmed. So, use this grounding technique if your anxiety or panic becomes so intense that you feel like giving up or running away.

# WHAT'S TRIGGERING YOUR PANIC?

Often, a single root cause for panic can't be identified. But what we can identify are things that cause your panic to flare up. Using what you've learned from the previous activities, think about what could be triggering your panic.

Look back at the situations you logged when you had your panic attacks. Identify any common details or themes that have come up in those situations. Review the fears you recognized as connected to your panic.

Can you spot any triggers related to those perceived threats? List all possible triggers here and add others as they occur to you:

_____

_____

_____

_____

_____

_____

_____

_____

_____

_____

_____

_____

_____

_____

_____

_____

_____

_____

_____

# PROGRESSIVE MUSCLE RELAXATION

Thinking about your triggers may have made you tense. Tension can be a symptom of or a trigger for panic. Progressive muscle relaxation (PMR) is a type of meditation that involves gradually and systematically focusing on different muscle groups, first tensing and then relaxing them.

This technique helps you continue to develop a stronger awareness of your body. It will help you notice tension as it builds. PMR also acts like a pendulum. If you tense first and then relax, you achieve a deeper level of relaxation than if you had just relaxed your muscles from a neutral point.

Remember, relaxation exercises should not be used to avoid panic, but you can practice PMR daily to lower your general level of stress as well as to prepare yourself to face your fears. Read along with the following script or record it to listen back to. Practice daily for about five to ten minutes. Be sure not to tense so tightly that you hurt yourself.

1. Sit or lie down. Curl your feet down or stretch them upward, focusing on the feeling of tension. Now relax, focusing on the feeling of relaxation.

2. Concentrate on your calf muscles, tensing them for a moment and then releasing the tension. Notice the difference in sensation.

3. Move your attention to your upper legs. To tense them, press your knees together, concentrating on the tension. Then relax, paying attention to the sensation.

4. Shift your focus to your torso, tensing your chest, back, and abdomen. Concentrate on the tightness without straining. And let the tension go, noticing the relaxation.

5. Now tense your arms from your shoulders to your hands. You can stretch them apart or press your hands together. Notice the tension. Then release, noticing the relaxation.

6. Scrunch up the muscles in your head and neck, pursing your lips together and squeezing your eyes shut. Then release, concentrating on the feeling of relaxation.

7. Now tense your whole body—all your muscles from your head to your feet. Then let it all go, allowing yourself to sink into the feeling of relaxation.

8. When you are ready, go back to your day.

# WEIGH THE PROS AND CONS

This week, you worked through some exercises to build your insight. You now have a better understanding of all the ways panic touches your life. With this in mind, list the pros and cons of addressing your panic with this seven-week plan here:

PROS

CONS

_____     _____

_____     _____

_____     _____

_____     _____

_____     _____

_____     _____

_____     _____

_____     _____

_____     _____

_____     _____

_____     _____

_____     _____

_____     _____

_____     _____

_____     _____

_____     _____

_____     _____

_____     _____

_____     _____

_____     _____

# LET'S REVIEW

What have you learned about your personal experience of panic that you didn't know before you started this workbook?

_____

_____

What are you ready to do to face your panic?

_____

_____

What has been helpful to practice over the last week?

_____

_____

What hasn't worked or what have you struggled with?

_____

_____

How will you use what you've learned moving forward?

_____

_____

*I can now identify my triggers so I can spot panic before it spirals out of control.*

# Key Takeaways

This week, you developed awareness of your body and emotions. You also began to track your panic attacks. Keep it up! You also explored how panic affects different areas of your life and identified factors that trigger it. What's more, you learned some tools to regulate your body when feeling overwhelmed. Here are this week's key takeaways:

- Becoming more connected and aware of your physical and emotional experience in a mindful way can help you better address it.

- Avoidance reinforces fear. It is important to recognize panic in the moment and track the details of your panic over time so you can understand and overcome it.

- Clarifying your triggers and what you perceive as threatening helps you problem-solve for the danger or challenge distorted thoughts that are telling you there's danger when none exists.

- Science-backed tools, such as breathing techniques and progressive muscle relaxation, can interrupt certain symptoms of panic. Do not use these tools to avoid your panic or anxiety; instead, use them to help you continue doing the work you need to do to face it.

- Use the tools that work for you on a consistent basis to manage your panic long-term.

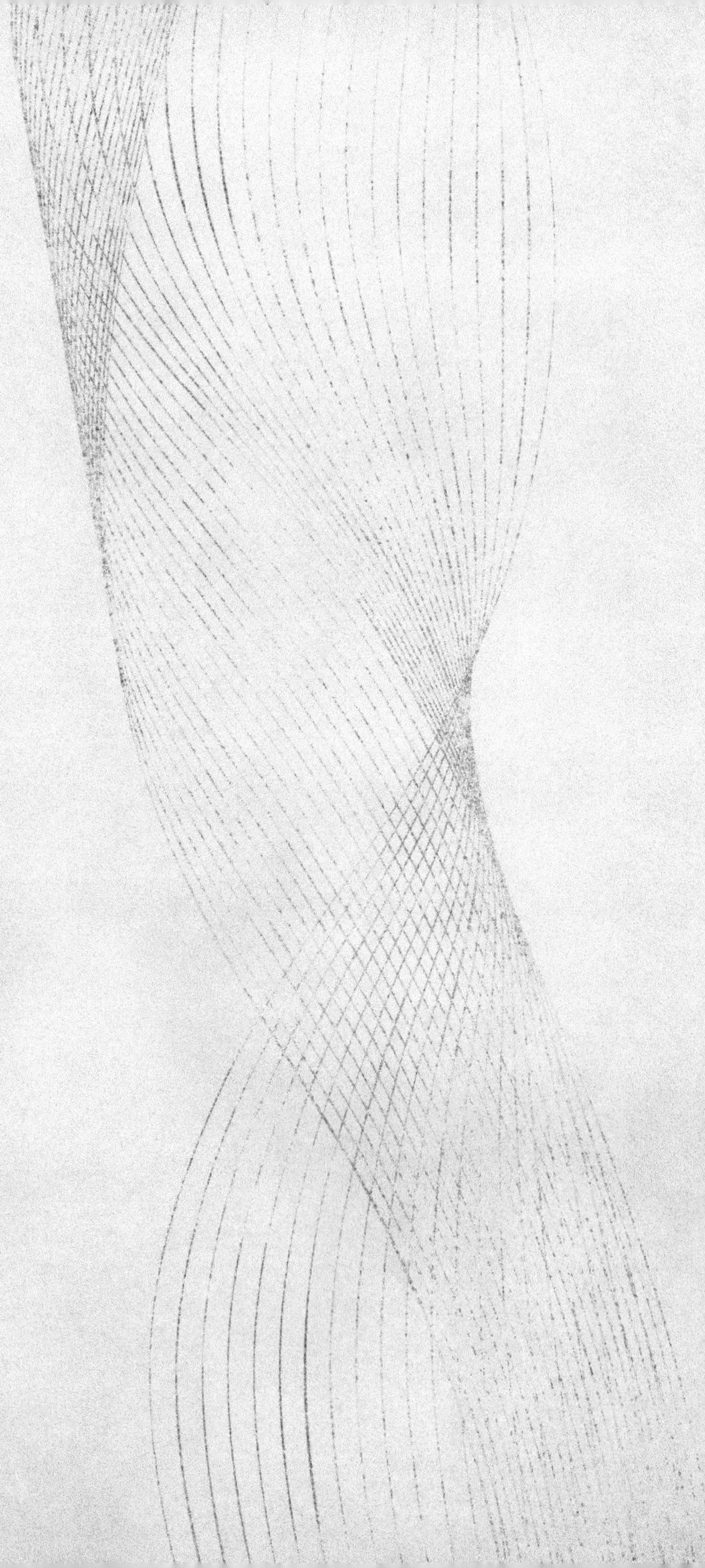

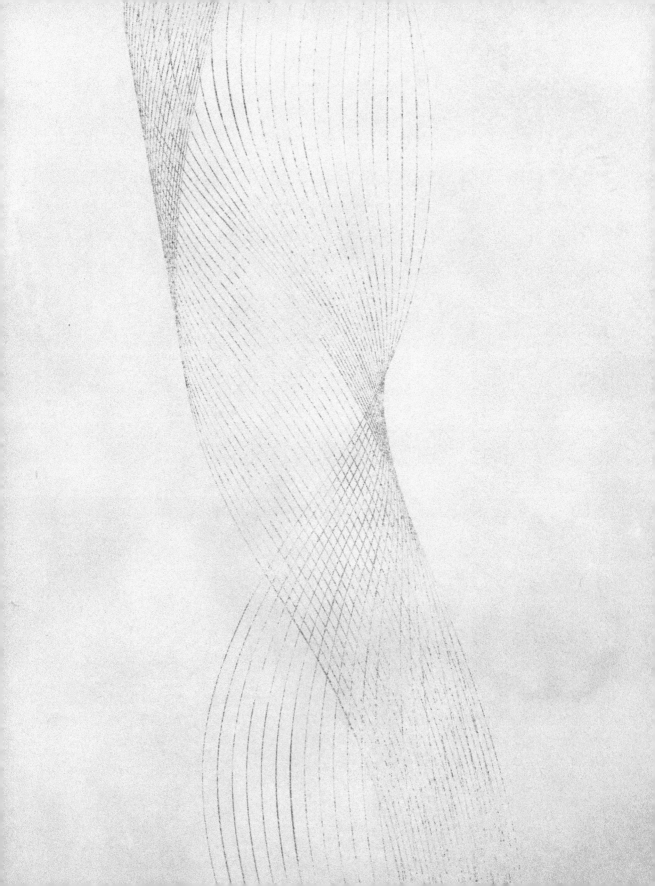

# Determine Your Needs and Goals

What do you want your life to look like? The activities this week will help you determine the answer to that question. You will be identifying your unique needs, developing personal goals, and assessing your lifestyle to set up helpful routines for things like sleep and exercise. This will help you define what you want your life to look like—from your relationships to your health.

As you do the work, you will get to know the different aspects of your cycle of panic, including your thoughts, sensations, and behaviors. You will also gain an intimate understanding of your physiology and what your body is telling you in the moment. You will learn practices to better understand your needs and continue to practice evidence-backed techniques to help you cope with whatever comes up. This will all culminate in a clear understanding of your goals, including the things you value and want to work toward.

Rini was running out of options. She was waiting at the academic advising office, anxiously picking at her cuticles. This was her first year of college. She had been so excited, looking forward to moving to a new country and getting to study her passion. But things had started to spiral quickly. The workload was demanding. Some of her classmates didn't have a social life at all; they just spent all their time studying.

Rini began to fall behind, overwhelmed not just by the work but also by her mounting worry that she wasn't cut out for this. And then she had a panic attack during an exam. It had been humiliating—and baffling. Rini hadn't grown up in a household where anyone talked about their feelings, so she was not prepared to handle panic. She didn't even have a name for it. What she did know was that she never wanted to go through that again.

That's when she started skipping classes, afraid another attack would strike when people were around to see. That didn't help with her studies, leading to dropping grades and more anxiety. She was then put on academic probation. The advisors said her academic performance would put her student visa in jeopardy.

Rini desperately wanted to stay in the country. She had dreams of becoming an engineer and making her parents proud. She knew what she needed was to be able to overcome her anxiety so she could go to class and be the amazing student she had always been. But she had no idea how to accomplish that. She felt stuck.

# Set Your Goals and State Your Needs

Getting clear on your needs and goals around panic is crucial to overcoming it. As you've learned, everyone's experience of panic is unique, so what you need for panic attack relief may be different from what someone else needs. Getting very specific about your goals will help you understand the changes that need to be made. Clarifying your needs and goals will make it easier to track your progress, to spot what is and is not working, and to reach out for help if necessary.

No goal is too big or small, and all your needs are valid. That is incredibly important to remember. Minimizing your needs or dismissing your goals will not help you achieve relief from panic attacks. Learning to develop a clear compass for your needs and goals will help you deal with your feelings head-on. Your thoughts, feelings, and sensations are all trying to convey something to you. They may be distorted at times, but ignoring them will not help you figure out what is real. The work you do this week will help you learn to listen to yourself.

## IMAGINE THE LIFE YOU WANT

Think about what your life would look like if you overcame your panic. Imagine that while you were sleeping, I waved a magic wand to solve all the problems you have around panic. As the days go by, you start noticing changes in your life. In this worksheet, describe these changes in each area.

| RELATIONSHIPS | SCHOOL/WORK |
|---|---|
| | |
| HEALTH | DAILY ACTIVITIES |
| | |

# WORK ON YOUR SLEEP ROUTINE

Panic and anxiety can lead to increased activation of your amygdala, which fires up your SNS, keeping you in an alert state to respond to danger. That state can make it difficult to relax enough to get to sleep properly. Worrisome thoughts that trigger your anxiety can also activate your SNS. Unfortunately, this can create a cycle that feeds into itself. Sleep deprivation can lead to increased amygdala activation, leading to a more intense anxiety response, leading to more sleep deprivation.

Adequate sleep can help lower the resting state of your amygdala, reducing your general stress level. Getting good sleep is essential to panic attack relief. Here are some tips to improve your sleep. Check off any you need to work on:

☐ Keep a consistent sleep schedule.

☐ Eliminate all light sources one hour before bed, including sources of blue light like your phone or TV.

☐ Save your bed for sleep and sex. Don't use it to engage in other activities like watching TV or doing work; when you do, you're conditioning your body to be alert in bed.

☐ Create a consistent relaxing ritual before bed, such as a meditation or a soothing self-care activity.

☐ Don't drink alcohol or caffeine close to bedtime.

☐ Don't engage in exercise too close to bedtime.

☐ Don't nap. Napping makes it harder for you to be appropriately tired at night.

☐ If you're struggling to sleep, engage in any kind of relaxation strategy such as deep breathing (see page 49) or progressive muscle relaxation (see page 53).

☐ If you still can't sleep after trying for a while, get out of bed and do something relaxing until you can.

Use this checklist to assess your sleep habits and slowly begin to make the changes necessary to reduce your anxiety and panic.

# KEEP A PANIC CYCLE RECORD

Panic is made up of three parts: (1) emotional and physical feelings, (2) thoughts, and (3) behaviors. In the panic cycle, feelings are your body's way of protecting itself. Thoughts are your perception of a real or imagined threat. Behaviors are how you respond to your panic.

Often when you are panicked or anxious, you are doing things that seem like they are reducing your anxiety or panic in the moment, but they are in fact intensifying and prolonging it in the long term.

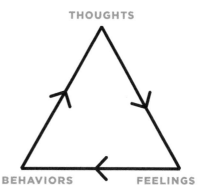

The panic cycle can begin at any of these points. Your thoughts can affect how you feel. Or the way you feel can affect your behaviors. Understanding the connection between your thoughts, emotional and physical feelings, and behaviors will help you learn what you need to better manage your panic.

This week, start recording details of your cycle any time you feel panic or anxiety. Here's an example:

## PANIC/ANXIETY CYCLE RECORD

| Date/ Time | Trigger | Thoughts | Feelings emotions and physical sensations | Behaviors |
|---|---|---|---|---|
| Monday, July 17th, at 2:00 p.m. | Meeting my partner's friends | I look weird.<br><br>I am not connected to my body.<br><br>Am I going crazy? | Panic<br><br>Shame<br><br>Blushing<br><br>Palms sweaty<br><br>Heart pounding<br><br>Hands tingling | Looking at my phone so I don't make eye contact with anyone<br><br>Going to the bathroom when I feel uncomfortable<br><br>Leaving early so I don't become panicked |

CONTINUED ▶

Use this log to keep a detailed record of your cycle each time it occurs:

## PANIC/ANXIETY CYCLE RECORD

| Date/ Time | Trigger | Thoughts | Feelings emotions and physical sensations | Behaviors |
| --- | --- | --- | --- | --- |
|  |  |  |  |  |

# SITTING WITH YOUR EMOTIONS

When you feel an emotion, your body generates a chemical response that flushes out of your system in less than ninety seconds. This shows us that all emotions are intended to have a beginning, a peak, and an end, as illustrated by figure 1.

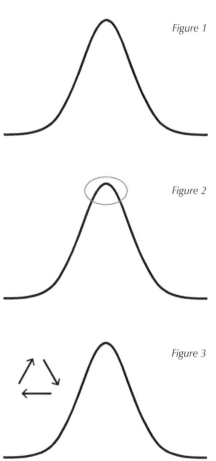

*Figure 1*

However, we can get stuck in an emotional loop in two ways. First, if we ruminate or overidentify with the feeling, those thoughts restimulate the emotion. That can look like "I'm a sad person. I'll be sad forever. This will never change." Notice how we get stuck at the peak, as illustrated by figure 2.

*Figure 2*

The second way we can get stuck is by avoidance. Emotions are intended to be messages to us, like physical pain. If I were to sprain my ankle, I'd pay attention to that pain and address it. If I didn't, that pain would increase, the message getting louder. Our emotions are similar. If we avoid an emotion, we may temporarily get relief, but the emotion often resurfaces, possibly getting more intense or coming out in unintended ways, bringing us back into the loop, as illustrated in figure 3.

*Figure 3*

The key to emotional regulation is to sit with your feelings in a mindful way, like this:

1. Allow yourself to recognize and feel the emotion, such as "I am sad right now. I feel heavy and tense."

2. Remind yourself it is temporary. "I feel this way right now, but I know it will pass in time."

3. Let it run its course.

Practice this regularly when you struggle with emotions. Label your emotion, mindfully notice your related sensations, and allow the feeling to be.

# WHAT ARE YOUR FEELINGS TELLING YOU?

You can get stuck in an emotional loop if avoidance or rumination prevents you from hearing the messages your feelings are trying to convey. Emotions inform us about what we need. You may be getting distorted messages, but ignoring a message doesn't make it go away. Being able to clearly recognize your emotions and the message they are conveying helps you create a plan to address them. Respond to these prompts:

What did you notice about allowing yourself to feel your feelings in the previous exercise? Did they get worse? Did you feel overwhelmed?

_____

_____

_____

_____

What do you think the emotion is trying to communicate to you?

_____

_____

_____

_____

*What we feel, we are able to heal.*
*What we resist persists.*

# SELF-COMPASSION PRACTICE

Figuring out your needs around panic can be hard. It may lead to critical self-talk. Self-compassion is a great tool to combat that negative voice in your head. Kristin Neff is at the forefront of research on self-compassion. She has developed various strategies you can use to practice self-compassion, and she defined *self-compassion* in a way that makes sense. For more on her work, see the Resources on page 184.

Self-compassion is made up of three parts: (1) mindfulness, (2) common humanity, and (3) kindness. Let's take a look:

1. You can't be compassionate with yourself unless you acknowledge you are suffering and allow yourself to *mindfully* feel difficult emotions.

2. Often when we struggle, we feel very isolated. But we all experience tough feelings like panic or shame. *Common humanity* involves reminding yourself that you are not alone and that suffering is a universal human experience.

3. The last step of self-compassion is to *be kind to yourself.* It can be hard to know where to begin. A good way to understand how to be kind to yourself is to think about someone you know going through your exact same struggle. Imagine what you would do to comfort them. Maybe you would offer them a hug or words of support. Then give that same support to yourself.

Think about any difficult experiences you're likely to encounter this week. When they occur, practice self-compassion.

# NOTICE THE EXCEPTIONS

You have done a lot of exploration on how panic affects you. It can also be helpful to recognize the exceptions. This reminds you that panic is not actually in control all the time and that you do have strengths that can be leveraged.

When is panic not affecting your life? What are the areas or situations where you don't struggle with panic? Describe them:

_____

_____

_____

_____

# PHYSICAL EXERCISE FOR PANIC

Do you exercise? Various research studies have shown that exercise can reduce anxiety or panic, so, if you don't do so regularly, you may want to begin, with your doctor's approval.

Exercise can affect your panic in several ways. Twenty minutes of aerobic exercise can lower the activation of your SNS and your amygdala, as well as burn off the chemicals released into your body during your panic response. And as you've learned, muscle tension increases anxiety. Exercise causes your muscles to relax, allowing your body to return to neutral. Regular physical exercise can reduce the resting state of your amygdala, lowering your body's reactivity to any possible triggers.

Here are a few ways to use exercise for your panic:

- Develop a regular routine of twenty minutes of aerobic exercise, such as running or water aerobics.

- Engage in yoga regularly, combining the benefits of deep breathing and muscle relaxation.

- Take regular walks.

- Engage in strength-training exercises.

Set aside time this week to fit exercise into your daily routine.

# DIAPHRAGMATIC BREATHING PRACTICE

Your diaphragm is a dome-shaped muscle at the base of your lungs. When you inhale, your diaphragm contracts and moves down, allowing your lungs to expand with air. We are all born with the ability to engage our diaphragm, but over time, we often lose the habit. Breathing from the chest, as many people do, is a shallower way of breathing that doesn't use the full capacity of the lungs and can contribute to chest tightness and overbreathing.

Diaphragmatic breathing works by consciously pulling your diaphragm down with each breath, allowing your lungs to expand more fully and efficiently. Follow these steps:

1. To feel your diaphragm, especially at first, it helps to lie on a flat surface like the floor.

2. Place one hand on your upper chest and the other just below your rib cage.

3. Inhale slowly, breathing down toward your stomach. You should feel your stomach expanding under your hand. Your chest should not move.

4. Exhale slowly, tensing your abdomen and feeling your stomach falling downward. Your chest should still not be moving.

5. Repeat for at least three to five minutes.

Engage in this breathing exercise three times each day this week. When you practice diaphragmatic breathing, don't try to force yourself to calm down. Remember that overbreathing is not harmful. Instead, use diaphragmatic breathing to regulate your breath while also leaning into your current feeling.

# CONNECT WITH YOUR PANIC QUIZ

You've learned a lot about the science of panic. Now let's test your knowledge so you can continue to develop a better understanding of what's happening in your body when you are panicking.

Review the list of physical symptoms of panic. Then review the reasons for these symptoms. For each of the reasons listed, write any associated physical symptoms in the correct column (some symptoms may appear more than once).

When you're done, check your answers against the answer key to see how much you know about your body. If you're still unsure, refer to "How Panic Affects the Body" on page 12 to refresh your memory. Understanding the changes in your body during panic can help you feel more prepared to engage in exposure in the future.

**Physical Symptoms**

- Muscle tension

- Shortness of breath

- Heart racing or pounding

- Sweating

- Upset stomach

- Tingling, numbness, or clamminess

- Feeling dizzy, lightheaded

- Confusion, derealization, depersonalization

- Shaking/trembling

- Negative thoughts

- Chest pain/tightness

**The Reasons**

- Preparing your body to spring into action (**Action**)

- Preventing you from overheating (**Regulating Temperature**)

- Energy/blood flow redirected to larger muscles (**Strength**)

- Brain shifting into threat detection (**Alert**)

| Action | Regulating Temperature | Strength | Alert |
|---|---|---|---|
|  |  |  |  |

# LET'S REFLECT

With a better understanding of what's happening inside your body, how do you feel about your physical symptoms now?

_____

_____

_____

_____

What surprised you most about your answers to the previous quiz?

_____

_____

_____

_____

How has this changed the way you think about panic?

_____

_____

_____

_____

# OBJECTIVE MONITORING PRACTICE

The way you monitor your experience matters. There are two different ways to observe an experience: subjectively and objectively.

1. **Subjective monitoring** involves self-reporting from your perspective, like an opinion instead of a fact. "I feel terrible" or "I can't handle this" are examples of subjective monitoring. This kind of monitoring is more likely to be extreme and tends to increase anxiety.

2. **Objective monitoring** is tracking the facts of your experience. An example could be "My heart is racing, my temperature is rising, and my palms are sweaty." This also involves recognizing the facts of the situation, such as "I am in a car that is not moving. There is no danger." Objective monitoring can help give you some space from the intensity of the situation. This allows you a pause to process and decide how you want to respond, instead of reacting immediately in the moment.

This week and beyond, whenever you feel an emotion you struggle with, monitor your experience objectively. Look at just the facts and state them to yourself. The more you practice, the less difficult this will become. Becoming more objective about your panic helps you identify your needs to better meet them in the moment.

# WHAT DO YOU VALUE?

What you care about the most gives you a good idea of your values. Are your family or romantic relationships the most important to you? Is being physically active a priority? Do you really care about advancing your career? With what you care about in mind, describe your values:

_____

_____

_____

_____

_____

_____

_____

_____

_____

_____

_____

_____

_____

_____

_____

_____

Our values motivate us to do things. However, avoiding panic and anxiety can often get in the way of our values. If you value your relationships but aren't spending time with your friends or family because of panic, you aren't living in line with your values. Continue working through this plan to help you change your relationship with panic and start reconnecting with your values.

# WHAT ARE YOUR GOALS?

Now that you have a clearer understanding of your needs and values, you can define your goals. When creating goals, be specific and concrete. It's also good to know how you will measure your progress. Thinking specifically of your goals for panic management, respond to these prompts:

What are your goals for the remaining five weeks? How will you track your progress?

_____

_____

_____

What are your goals in the next six months? How will you track your progress?

_____

_____

_____

What are your long-term goals? How will you track your progress?

_____

_____

_____

How will you know when you have achieved your goals?

_____

_____

_____

# CREATING VALUES AFFIRMATIONS

Building off your goals and what you value, brainstorm some statements to remind yourself why you're doing this work. You can record these statements on your phone and listen back, if you'd like, or send them as texts to yourself to look back on and read aloud.

When things get difficult or uncomfortable or you are considering giving up, use these statements to reconnect with your motivation. For example, you can say, "I value family, and I want to travel to visit them." Or "I value music, and I want to enjoy concerts."

When you are struggling to engage in the exercises in this workbook or activities outside of it, repeat these statements to yourself.

*By facing my panic, I can get back to doing the things I care about.*

## Key Takeaways

This week, you have actively built your awareness of your needs, values, and goals. It takes bravery to do that. Acknowledge all your hard work. To support that work, here are the key takeaways:

- Getting clear on your needs, values, and goals will help you track your progress, identify what works and what doesn't, and reach out for help if necessary.

- Your lifestyle affects your panic. Sleep and exercise can reduce your anxiety in the long term. Developing a healthy sleep and exercise routine is crucial to panic attack management.

- Panic is made up of emotional and physical feelings, thoughts about the real or imagined threat, and behaviors that relieve or intensify it. Understanding the connection between your thoughts, feelings, and behaviors will help you learn what you need in the moment.

- You can get stuck in an emotional loop if you overidentify or ruminate on your emotions. You can also get stuck if you avoid emotions. All emotions are meant to pass in time. The key to emotional regulation is learning to mindfully experience emotions instead of resisting them.

- Avoiding anxiety and panic can stop us from doing the things we care about. Use your values affirmations when you are struggling to reconnect with your motivation for change.

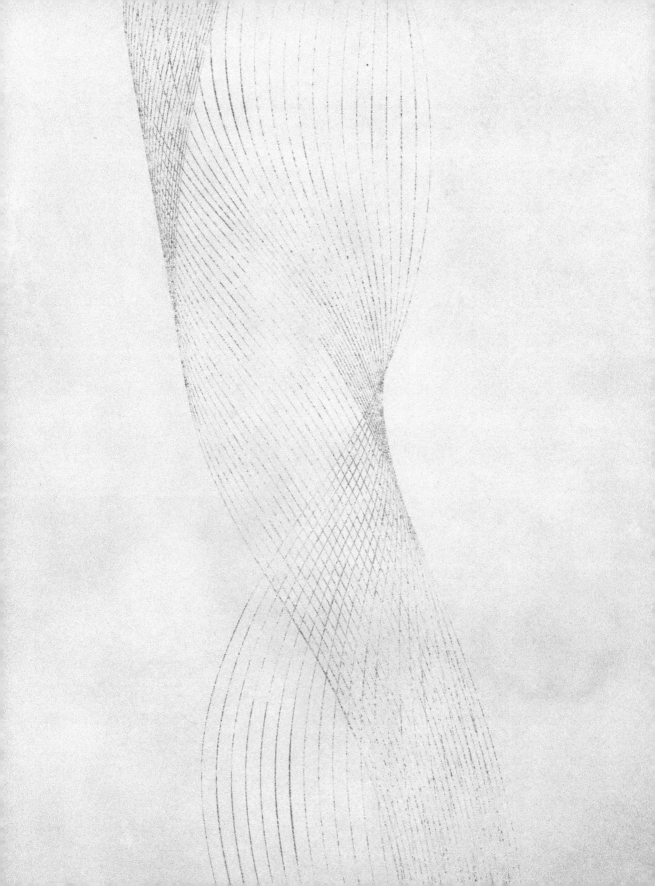

# Identify Where You Struggle

This week, you will explore the ways you struggle. You will learn about your challenges and the barriers standing in your way, including the aspects of your panic that have been the hardest to cope with. Understanding the specifics of your struggles will help you learn what you need to address to overcome panic. There are also exercises to help you distinguish between your thoughts and feelings so you can validate your feelings and, later, use tools to reframe any distorted thoughts.

Panic behaviors can be tricky. There are certain behaviors that might seem like they're helping in the moment but are actually exacerbating your panic. The exercises and activities this week will help you spot those behaviors and understand how they relate to your fears so you can interrupt unhelpful cycles. You will also explore your relationship to your body and how physical sensations themselves are triggering or feeding into your panic. There will be some strategies that work for you and some that don't connect at all. This is where accountability is key. You will get better at recognizing what is effective and keep using those skills to overcome your panic.

Darnell was trying hard not to concentrate on the sweat dripping down his back. He tried not to think about the massive wet stain that would be on his shirt when he got off the bus.

He was on a road trip with his friend Jimmy. Jimmy was gabbing away, pointing out the landmarks and talking about what they'd do when they arrived. They were on a weeklong vacation to visit national parks. His buddy had found a great deal for an all-inclusive trip. They were really into rock climbing and being in nature, so it had seemed like a perfect fit—or it had to Jimmy.

The moment Darnell thought about being stuck on a bus for hours with no way to escape, his stomach dropped. But Jimmy didn't know that Darnell struggled with panic attacks. Darnell had never told him that enclosed spaces made him feel out of control. So, he had agreed to the trip, praying he wouldn't have an attack.

Darnell had just started seeing a new therapist, so he knew the plan was to eventually face his fears. But he definitely did not feel ready right now. He gripped his hands on his lap to prevent them from shaking, feeling somehow tense all over and also like he was floating, getting more and more disconnected from the moment. He gritted his teeth to steady himself against a wave of dizziness. He didn't know how he was going to survive this trip. He hoped what he had learned in therapy so far would be enough.

# Get Clear on Your Challenges

As you know, panic can take many forms. Understanding your struggles with panic will help you ensure your relief plan caters to your specific needs. If there are resources missing in your life, such as time or money, identifying those barriers will help you work toward resolving them.

Without understanding your personal challenges, you might keep trying something you learned should be effective. If your efforts weren't successful, you might give up altogether. You may even internalize the failure as some sign that nothing will change or there is something uniquely wrong with you that can't be fixed. That doesn't have to be true. Your specific struggles with panic can act as a guide pointing toward what you need to address to finally overcome it. This week, you will develop insight into those challenges.

## WHAT'S HOLDING YOU BACK?

Maybe it was hard to admit you deal with panic attacks. Maybe you hate the idea of asking for help. Perhaps you think you should be able to just grin and bear it. There are likely barriers standing in your way, preventing you from overcoming your panic. Think about them now.

Describe whatever is holding you back from dealing with your panic (e.g., fear, time, or money):

_____

_____

_____

_____

What could you do to address those barriers?

_____

_____

_____

_____

# THOUGHTS VERSUS FEELINGS QUIZ

Your feelings are always valid. They reflect what you are going through at the time. But your thoughts might not be rational, especially when you are panicking. Differentiating between your thoughts and feelings will later help you notice and respond in a more helpful way to any distorted thoughts that might be triggering your panic.

Have you struggled to distinguish between a thought and a feeling? That's normal. Even the way we talk can make it a bit confusing. Someone might say "I feel ugly." But "ugly" is not a feeling. In this example, this person is *thinking* they are ugly, and that's likely causing them uncomfortable *emotions*, such as embarrassment or panic.

As a reminder, an emotion is a temporary, subjective state of being, often described with one word, and often accompanied by physical sensations. A thought is a statement, comment, or observation you make about yourself, others, or the world around you.

Mark whether each of these statements is a thought or a feeling:

| | | |
|---|---|---|
| **I am a failure.** | Thought | Feeling |
| **I am angry.** | Thought | Feeling |
| **I feel like something bad is going to happen.** | Thought | Feeling |
| **I am nervous.** | Thought | Feeling |
| **I feel ashamed.** | Thought | Feeling |
| **I can't handle this.** | Thought | Feeling |
| **I feel like I am dying.** | Thought | Feeling |
| **I am annoyed.** | Thought | Feeling |
| **I feel out of control.** | Thought | Feeling |
| **I feel like an inconvenience.** | Thought | Feeling |
| **I am upset.** | Thought | Feeling |
| **I feel excited.** | Thought | Feeling |
| **I feel embarrassed.** | Thought | Feeling |
| **I am going crazy.** | Thought | Feeling |

Were you clear on the difference between thoughts and feelings? Has confusing them affected your panic?

_____

_____

_____

_____

# HOW WELL DO YOU KNOW YOUR PANIC?

You've been doing a lot of work to better understand your panic. Let's dig a little deeper:

How often are you experiencing panic attacks?

_____

_____

_____

How much time do you spend worrying about your attacks?

_____

_____

_____

Do you always know what triggered them or do they happen out of the blue?

_____

_____

_____

Do you ever have panic attacks that wake you from sleeping? If so, how often?

_____

_____

_____

On a scale of one to ten, how uncomfortable or intense are your attacks?

_____

_____

_____

# SPOT YOUR OVERBREATHING

There are a few different ways you may be overbreathing:

* You could be hyperventilating in the most obvious way: breathing in lots of air quickly, as though you are panting. This is likely to happen during a moment of panic.

* Your breathing could be affected in slight, less noticeable ways, such as sighing or yawning. Sighing and yawning can happen when you feel a strong feeling, such as anxiety.

* You may be in the habit of chronic mild overbreathing; you may take in one or two big breaths during a moment of stress or just be overbreathing slightly in your daily activities. Chronic overbreathing can cause more mild symptoms of anxiety such as trouble concentrating and lightheadedness, which may make you more susceptible to panic during a stressful moment. Mild overbreathing can also lower your body's ability to deal with changes in your breathing. A slight change can then trigger panic, possibly causing a panic attack that feels like it's coming out of the blue.

This week, practice noticing your breathing to be aware of when overbreathing is happening. A balanced rate of breathing is about ten to fourteen breaths per minute. When you become aware of overbreathing, practice the diaphragmatic breathing techniques on page 69 and the deep breathing techniques on page 49 to bring your breath back into balance.

# WHAT ARE YOUR BIGGEST STRUGGLES?

What do you find hardest about facing or dealing with your panic? Are you struggling to identify your triggers? Feel your feelings? Do you truly believe your life can be different? Describe those struggles:

_____

_____

_____

_____

_____

How might these struggles hinder your panic attack management plan?

_____

_____

_____

_____

_____

*Struggling is a human experience.*
*My struggle does not mean*
*I can't overcome panic.*

# SELF-COMPASSION MEDITATION

Focusing on how you struggle with panic is challenging. You might be spiraling right now, fixating on all the reasons you feel stuck. Pause here to remind yourself that compassion is the drive to alleviate suffering. So, self-compassion is exactly what you need right now.

Here is a script for a self-compassion meditation you can use, adapted from Kristin Neff's "Self-Compassion Break," from her Mindful Self-Compassion (MSC) program. Follow along as you meditate or listen back to your recording.

1. Find a comfortable place where you can be undisturbed for five minutes.

2. Bring to mind a current struggle and focus on the details.

3. Notice the feelings this brings up. Allow yourself to experience these difficult feelings. Recognize that this is a moment of suffering.

4. Find words that speak to you about this suffering. Maybe "I'm going through a hard time right now" or "I'm really struggling."

5. Now remind yourself that you are not alone in these feelings. Struggles are a natural part of being human.

6. Focus in on where you feel this feeling the strongest. Place a hand right on that spot. Send yourself warmth and support with your touch.

7. Imagine a close friend is sitting in front of you, telling you they're going through the exact same thing. What would you say to them? Maybe "That sounds really hard, but you're going to be okay" or "Whatever happens, I'm here for you." Then say those words to yourself.

Resilience is the ability to bounce back from challenges. Self-compassion has been shown to increase resilience. To support your ability to bounce back from panic, practice this meditation any time you are struggling.

# IDENTIFY YOUR SAFETY BEHAVIORS

Safety behaviors are any behaviors you engage in to feel safe that may lower your panic in the moment but aren't logically solving the problem. Think about safety behaviors like a security blanket a child carries around. The blanket doesn't actually make the child safe; it just temporarily relieves their anxiety while also reinforcing that what they are afraid of (e.g., the dark) is dangerous.

Here are examples of safety behaviors. Check off any you use and add others that come to mind.

- ☐ Looking at your phone to avoid feeling anxious

- ☐ Keeping a water bottle with you to avoid nausea or dry mouth

- ☐ Carrying around superstitious objects like a special keychain

- ☐ Only going places with someone else

- ☐ Distraction

- ☐ Avoidance

- ☐ Bringing something to read to avoid feeling anxious

- ☐ Talking on the phone to avoid anxiety

- ☐ Carrying around medication, even if you don't intend to take it

- ☐ Not making eye contact

- ☐ Overpreparing (so you're not anxious when the unexpected happens)

- ☐ Overcontrolling

- ☐ Reassurance seeking (turning to someone else to ease your fears when there is no actual threat or you already know the information)

- ☐ Other: _____

- ☐ Other: _____

# IDENTIFY YOUR FEARS

Safety behaviors keep you in the cycle of panic because turning to them feeds into your fear. To see how, choose a few of your safety behaviors and write them in the first column, record the fear you think causes them in the second column, and then respond to the prompts.

| Safety Behavior | Fear |
| --- | --- |
| *Example: Bringing someone with you* | *If I have a panic attack alone, I could get seriously hurt.* |
| | |
| | |
| | |
| | |

CONTINUED ▸

How did you feel while identifying your fears?

_____

_____

_____

_____

Turning to safety behaviors reinforces the belief that a perceived threat is, in fact, dangerous. They also trick you into underestimating your own capacity to cope. For example, if someone is afraid of flying and keeps a Xanax in her carry-on but does not take it, she might attribute her lack of panic to having the Xanax on hand, even though she got through the flight on her own. This becomes a vicious cycle of dependence, making you believe you need your safety behaviors and increasing your anxiety if you can't use them. Worst of all, they prevent you from finding out if your fears would really come true.

Take a moment to imagine your fears coming true. Are your safety behaviors truly protecting you from them?

_____

_____

_____

_____

If your fear happened, how would you cope?

_____

_____

_____

_____

# GET TO THE ROOT OF YOUR FEARS

To eventually face and overcome your fear, you need to be able to understand the root of it. If I asked you what scares you about panic attacks, you might say, "They're uncomfortable." But that doesn't get to the core of your fear. Why are they uncomfortable? Are you afraid you'll be uncomfortable and get stuck like that? Are you afraid that discomfort will make you lose your mind?

Understanding the core of your fear will help you challenge and confront it. The downward arrow technique can help you get to the root of your fears. Start with the first thing that popped into your mind as a fear related to your panic. Then investigate that thought with clarifying questions. Here's an example:

I will be uncomfortable.

What about the discomfort is scary?

I am afraid it will go on forever.

If that were true, what's scary about that?

I'm afraid I won't be able to handle it.

If you weren't able to handle it, what would happen?

I'd get so overwhelmed and distracted I'd hurt myself or someone else.

I could have an accident while driving.

CONTINUED ▶

Now it's your turn to try this technique. Here are some helpful questions to ask yourself:

- If that were true, what does it mean or what would happen next?
- What about that is scary or distressing?
- What does that mean about you, your future, your relationships?
- Why does that bother you?

**Fearful thought**

_____

**Question**

_____

**Fearful thought**

_____

**Question**

_____

**Fearful thought**

_____

**Question**

_____

**Fearful thought**

_____

# DETAIL YOUR ANXIETY FEEDBACK LOOP

We've talked a lot about external triggers for panic, but your internal sensations can also become a trigger, as in the case of panic disorder. For example, Steph is having dinner with a coworker, feeling perfectly at ease. Then she gets a call that her daughter is in detention. This makes her a little anxious, causing muscle tension and increased heart rate. Then she gets in her car to drive home. Someone cuts her off, making her angry and raising her blood pressure. The next moment, Steph is having a panic attack. Her physical symptoms created an anxiety feedback loop. Steph was not particularly afraid of driving, but her physical symptoms primed her body to respond with panic when she experienced her next stressor.

Your brain can interpret your physical sensations as a sign of danger, activating your SNS. Here's how it looks:

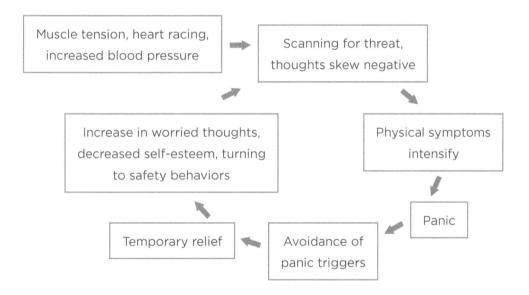

Think about some of your panic attacks. Can you identify physical symptoms that caused an anxiety feedback loop?

_____

_____

CONTINUED▶

Detail your anxiety feedback loop here:

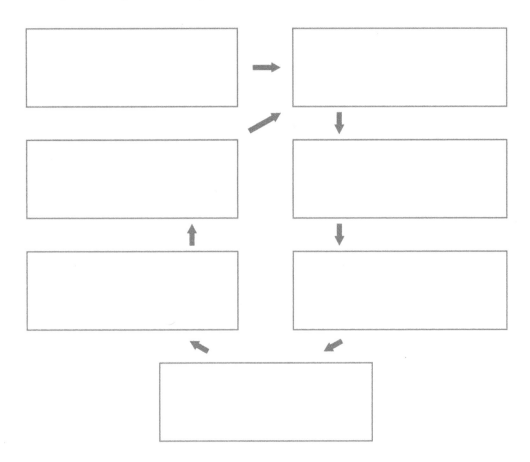

# MEASURE YOUR FEAR

A key aspect of panic disorder is a fear of fear. Many people aren't even aware that they are afraid of panic attacks but instead just feel sensitive to certain physical sensations. It's important to understand the degree and nature of this fear in order to confront it. Rate the intensity of your fear or discomfort on a scale of zero to ten, for each symptom of panic:

| Sensation | Fear/Discomfort Rating |
|---|---|
| Heart pounding or racing | |
| Sweating | |
| Trembling or shaking | |
| Shortness of breath or feelings of being smothered | |
| Feelings of choking | |
| Chest pain or discomfort | |
| Nausea or upset stomach | |
| Feeling dizzy, unsteady, lightheaded, or faint | |
| Hot or cold flashes | |
| Paresthesia (numbness or tingling, especially in the hands or feet) | |

CONTINUED ▶

| Sensation | Fear/Discomfort Rating |
|---|---|
| Derealization (a surreal, "off" feeling) | |
| Depersonalization (feeling detached from yourself, including an out-of-body experience) | |
| Thinking you are losing control | |
| Thinking you are dying | |
| Thinking you are going crazy | |

What did you learn from this exercise?

_____

_____

_____

_____

_____

_____

_____

_____

_____

_____

_____

_____

_____

# WHAT ARE YOUR SYMPTOM-BASED FEARS?

If you develop a fear of a physical symptom, avoiding that symptom could start a negative cycle—reinforcing your fear that the symptom is a sign of danger.

Which symptom is the hardest for you to face?

_____

_____

_____

What about that symptom makes you uncomfortable or afraid? Do you fear it is a sign of something more serious? Describe the reasons for your fear:

_____

_____

_____

# WHAT HASN'T WORKED?

Describe the actions you took and the strategies you used to manage your panic—before you started this workbook—that have *not* worked.

_____

_____

_____

For each, describe why you think it didn't work:

_____

_____

_____

# MAKE A COPING CARD

In the upcoming weeks, you will be facing things you struggle with. There will be moments that are hard and moments when you're tempted to give up. During these times, a coping card is a resource you can use for support to keep going.

In addition to this example, there's a blank coping card for you to fill in at the end of this exercise. Copy it over to an index card or take a photo with your phone of the one you fill in. The idea is to keep it with you at all times. On the blank coping card, write the following (being as brief as possible):

> *By facing my panic, I can get back to doing the things I care about.*
>
> *Exercise*
>
> *Mindfulness*
>
> *I want to make new friends.*
>
> *Objective monitoring*
>
> *Deep, diaphragmatic breathing*
>
> *I want to go on work trips.*
>
> *Panic is natural and is not here to harm me.*
>
> *Self-compassion*

- Your values

- Things you want to do that panic has been holding you back from

- Helpful affirmations

- Anything that could help you while you are struggling, like kind words or facts you've learned that make you feel more confident

- Activities you want to regularly practice, like exercise or meditation

Get in the habit of looking at your coping card often to remind yourself of useful strategies to manage your panic. You will learn more tools as you continue through this plan. Add any that work for you as you go on.

# LET'S REVIEW

What have you learned about your personal struggle with panic?

_____

_____

_____

_____

How will your new understanding help you cope with your panic in healthy ways?

_____

_____

_____

_____

*Getting a better understanding of my struggles with panic will help me face them.*

# Key Takeaways

You have just cultivated insight into your struggles. Here are key takeaways for you to remember:

- Understanding your challenges gives you a clearer understanding of your needs. Because your experience of panic is unique, discovering what works for you and letting go of what doesn't is necessary for panic attack relief.

- Physical sensations can become a trigger and create a feedback loop, enhancing your sense of anxiety or panic. Your fear of physical sensations (and resulting behaviors) could be reinforcing the idea that the symptom itself is a sign of danger. Understanding your relationship to your body's sensations and how they could be feeding into your panic will help you learn to interrupt the cycle.

- Always validate your feelings. Distinguishing between your thoughts and feelings will help you notice and respond in a more helpful way to thoughts that could trigger your panic.

- Safety behaviors give you a false sense of security. Turning to them reinforces the belief that your perceived threat is truly dangerous, creating a cycle of dependence on these behaviors. They also trick you into underestimating your ability to cope and prevent you from finding out if your fears would really come true.

- Self-compassion is meant for difficult moments, improving your ability to bounce back. You can also use tools like diaphragmatic breathing to regulate your breathing and confront your fears instead of avoiding them. A coping card can remind you of helpful strategies or affirmations for support when you are struggling.

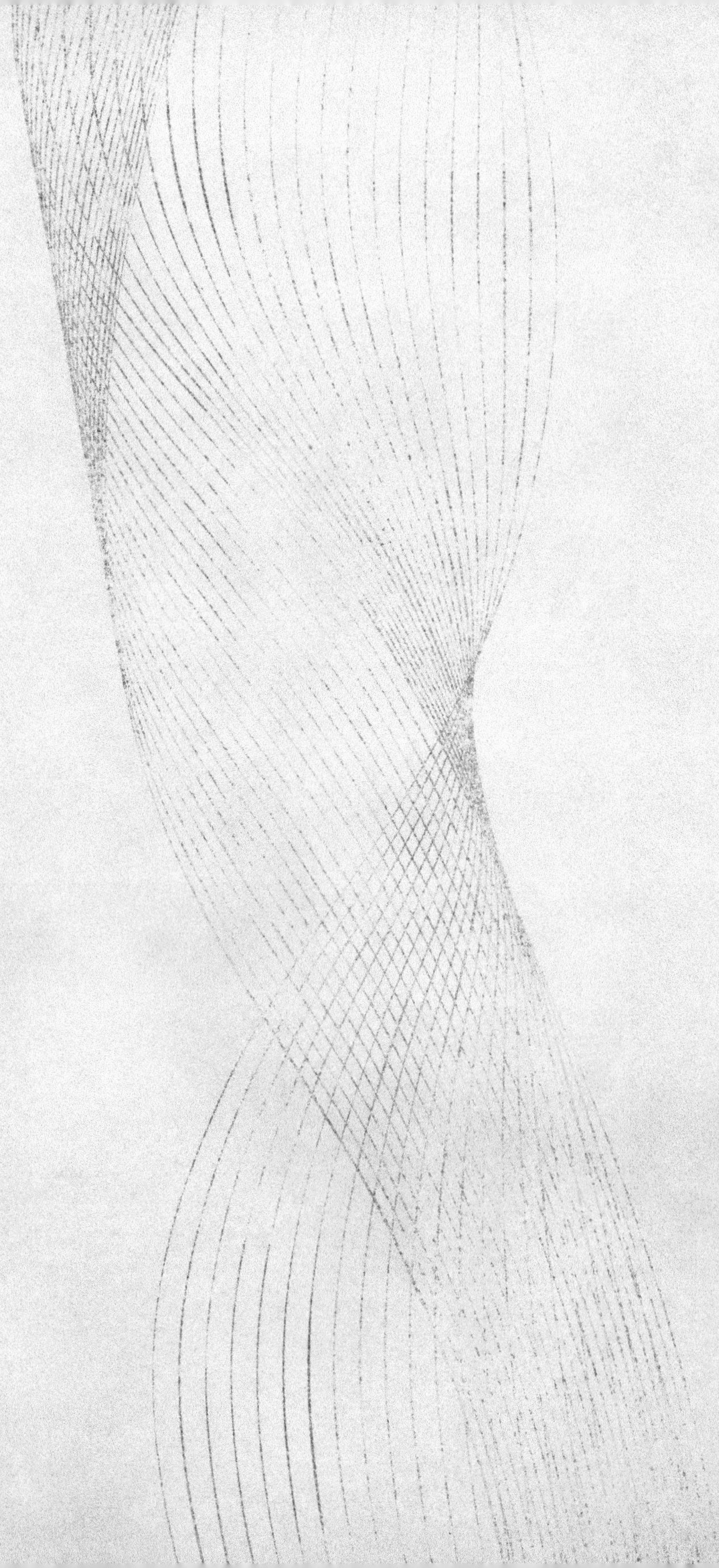

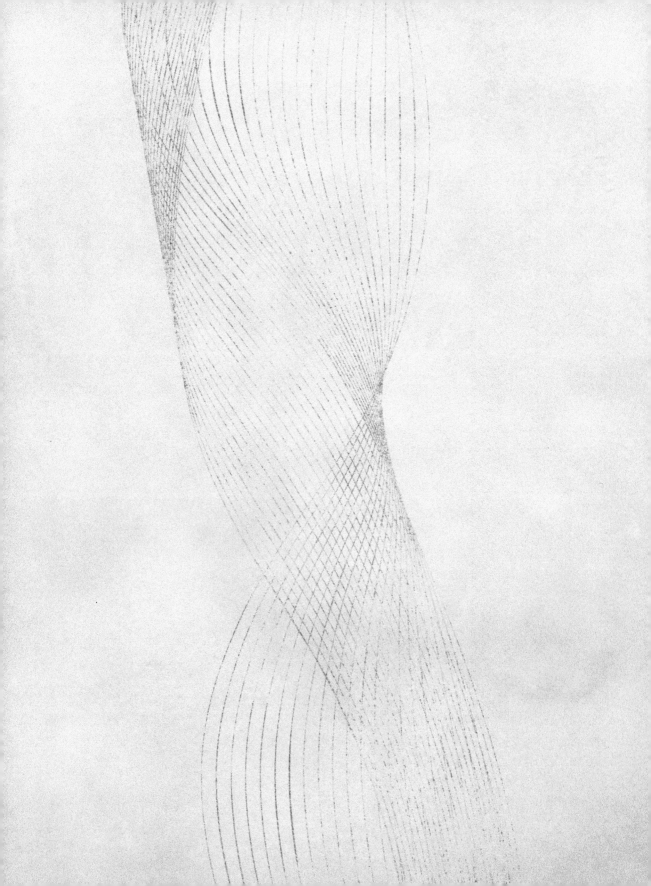

# Break Negative Thought Cycles

Your thoughts can trigger panic. But guess what? They can also reduce it. That's why you will focus on exploring your thought patterns this week. By learning about your own beliefs surrounding panic and debunking a few myths, you will be able to view your panic more realistically. Many kinds of thoughts intensify panic, such as anticipatory anxiety and jumping to worst-case scenarios. The way you relate to your thoughts can also affect your panic. If you get caught up in unhelpful worries, you can get anxious for no reason.

This week, you will learn to spot unhelpful thoughts and untwist them. You will also learn to evaluate your thoughts to plan for any real danger and shift your attention from distorted, unhelpful worries. These skills will help you stop distorted thoughts from spiraling out of control. You will then be able to reframe your thoughts with more helpful, balanced alternatives.

Nassim felt like he was going crazy. He sat in his living room, trying to force himself to draw the curtains. He told himself he had to face the day. He used to love meeting new people and feeling connected to his community. But then the first attack happened. He had been in the middle of a conversation when he felt his whole body start to shake. Then came the sense that time was slowing down. He felt like a stranger in his own body, watching himself but unable to connect with his sensations.

The experience had deeply disturbed him. Nassim had no frame of reference, nothing to explain the intense unease and bizarre symptoms. As the attacks continued, he concluded that he was slowly losing his mind. He became terrified of these moments. He couldn't bear the idea that others would find out. He constantly worried that he would lose control in public. Nassim had two children. What if someone realized and reported him? What if they took his children away from him?

The only solution Nassim could come up with was to hide. He didn't trust therapists and was too ashamed to speak to anyone he knew about it. He sent his kids on short errands and used delivery services for necessities like groceries. But he knew this wasn't sustainable. He tried to make himself believe this would pass. He should be strong enough. He should be able to interact with the world and provide for his family. But he couldn't bring himself to move. The thought of going outside and making eye contact with others kept him frozen on the couch. Everything felt overwhelming.

# How Negative Thought Patterns Exacerbate Panic

Your thoughts are how you interpret your experience, and how you interpret an experience affects your emotions and behaviors. Sometimes they are accurate. But sometimes our minds register threats that don't exist. It doesn't matter; it still sets off your nervous system. Your heart rate increases, your breathing quickens, and your muscles tense. It feels like a lion is stalking you.

If you don't spot your distorted thoughts, you can get stuck in a cycle of panic. One negative thought leads to another, rapidly escalating your fear. When we are in a state of anxiety or panic, our thoughts tend to become more negative because we are searching for a threat. Your mind will do everything it can to find one, including inflating worst-case scenarios or turning inward, finding innocent internal signals such as tingling in your limbs as serious signs of possible harm.

Being able to tell the difference between accurate thoughts and distorted ones is necessary for panic attack relief. If you really are in danger, you can develop an effective plan to prepare for that danger, instead of avoiding the issue and increasing the chances of something bad happening. If you spot irrational thoughts as they come up, you can separate yourself from them and respond with a more realistic perspective to stop the negative cycle before it overwhelms you.

## IDENTIFY TRUTHS ABOUT PANIC

There are several common myths about panic that may be worsening your anxiety. Let's weed out what's false from what's true. For each statement about panic, circle either true or false.

1. **Panic attacks cause heart attacks.**  True  False

2. **A panic attack is a temporary experience that will pass.**  True  False

3. **A panic attack will make me go crazy.**  True  False

4. **A panic attack can make me lose control.**  True  False

5. **Panic is a natural, universal emotion.**  True  False

6. **My brain can misinterpret a physical symptom as a sign of danger.**  True  False

7. **Panic will make me faint.**  True  False

8. **Panic attacks can cause some other life-threatening illness.**  True  False

9. **Most panic attacks last fewer than twenty minutes.**  True  False

CONTINUED ▸

10. **I need some degree of anxiety and fear to protect me from real danger.** .................................................... True      False

11. **Panic can go on forever.** .......................................................... True      False

12. **Panic attacks are uncomfortable but not dangerous.** ...... True      False

13. **To prevent panic, I should avoid all my triggers.** ................ True      False

**ANSWER KEY**

**True:** *2, 5, 6, 9, 10, 12*

**False:** *1, 3, 4, 7, 8, 11, 13*

If you answered *true* for any false statements, think about what you were taught about yourself or the world that influences your experience of panic. Were you raised to believe the world is a dangerous place? Or that you should always be in control of your body? Were you taught that intense emotions are bad or dangerous? Describe those beliefs:

_____

_____

_____

_____

_____

_____

_____

_____

_____

_____

_____

# WHAT ARE YOUR NEW BELIEFS?

Because the symptoms of panic can be so unsettling and confusing, coming to some false conclusions is understandable. However, learning to manage your panic also involves challenging any mistaken beliefs. Let's challenge a few now:

**Panic attacks will not make you go crazy.** The changes that occur in your body to protect you during a panic attack can cause symptoms that feel disturbing and may distort your sense of reality, such as depersonalization or derealization. Depersonalization can cause you to feel numbness, like you're observing yourself from outside of your body, and a feeling of detachment. Derealization can cause a surreal, dreamlike feeling and distortions in your sense of time and your surroundings. These symptoms can be uncomfortable but are harmless and do not mean your sanity will be compromised.

What do you think about this belief now?

_____

_____

_____

_____

**Panic attacks also do not cause a loss of control.** You may *feel* out of control because your body is undergoing the symptoms of panic, but you are still able to function. During panic, your muscles are actually more capable of movement and your responses have sped up. Recall times when you pulled over while driving, left quickly, or something else along those lines because of your panic. Those are examples of *being in control*; you took the steps you felt were necessary to protect yourself.

What do you think about this belief now?

_____

_____

_____

_____

CONTINUED ▶

**Your panic attack is not a sign of a heart attack or any other serious illness.** Heart attacks do share some common symptoms with panic attacks, such as shortness of breath and chest pain. You should get a physical evaluation to rule out any physical issues. But if your doctor has told you your heart is operating normally, the symptoms of a panic attack will not cause a heart attack. In fact, the symptoms are showing you that your heart is functioning correctly.

What do you think about this belief now?

_____

_____

_____

_____

**Fainting during an attack is very rare.** During a panic attack, you may feel dizzy or lightheaded, but fainting is more likely to happen because your blood pressure is low. When you experience panic, your blood pressure will probably rise, making it unlikely you will be in the appropriate state to faint.

What do you think about this belief now?

_____

_____

_____

_____

# AWARENESS OF ANTICIPATORY ANXIETY

Panic has probably led you to experience anticipatory anxiety. This includes the physical sensations of anxiety (such as muscle tension, restlessness, and trouble concentrating) and the worried thoughts about possible negative outcomes. You may spend a lot of your time worrying about a future panic attack. You may also worry about the consequences of an attack, such as how it will affect your health or impact your performance.

Now that you have built a stronger awareness of your panic, every day this week, practice noticing your anticipatory anxiety. Label it by saying something like "that's my anticipatory anxiety" or "those are my worried thoughts." Recognize that this is your amygdala trying to tell you that what you are facing is dangerous. Try to notice and not resist the anxiety. This anxiety is normal. It may be uncomfortable, but it won't hurt you. And remember that facing anxiety without trying to get away from it is teaching your brain that you can handle it, so your brain can learn it doesn't have to keep activating your nervous system to protect you from panic.

What did you notice about the thoughts you were having? How did they change each day?

_____

_____

_____

_____

_____

_____

# BEING WITH YOUR THOUGHTS

Much like other triggers for your panic, you may have tried to stop your negative thoughts. Unfortunately, research has shown that attempting to escape negative thoughts does not work. Let's try an experiment to test this out: Don't think of a white bear.

Did that white bear pop up immediately? Suppressing a thought, like trying to suppress your emotions, causes a rebound effect. This is because when you attempt to not think a thought, you are creating a connection with it. Also, when you are trying to avoid a thought, a part of your mind becomes extra vigilant for it. Checking in to make sure you are not thinking the thought actually brings it up in your mind. For example, if you see a white tablecloth, that might remind you that you're trying not to think of that bear, bringing it into your consciousness again.

Instead, this week, practice being with your thoughts in a nonjudgmental, mindful way. Allow yourself to notice negative thoughts as they arise, then let them naturally float away. Imagine that each of your thoughts is a train coming into the station. Like trains in a station, you cannot control your thoughts. You can board the "train" of your thought and get caught up in it. But just like a train, all thoughts leave in time. Notice the thought as it arrives. And instead of following the thought and engaging with it by analyzing or ruminating on it, acknowledge, "This is a thought," and observe it as it leaves.

This may be uncomfortable, especially at first. It can act like a form of exposure. If you allow yourself to think your thoughts and accept that they are *just thoughts*, not necessarily predictions of the future or defining who you are, over time, that discomfort can lessen and the frequency of those thoughts can reduce.

How does it feel to be with your thoughts?

_____

_____

_____

_____

# IDENTIFY THINKING ERRORS

We all have automatic thoughts, or thoughts that arise quickly in the moment, some-times without our even being aware of them. Many of these thoughts are negative and irrational. Some are just random. Some are like shortcuts. We take these shortcuts to make quicker evaluations. If a car is speeding my way, I don't have the time to measure its velocity or the angle of its approach. I am going to jump to a conclusion, "That car is going to hit me," and run out of the way. Jumping to conclusions is an example of the thinking shortcuts we take. These shortcuts are intended to protect us. But they can also lead to mistakes. What if the car wasn't going to hit me, but I rushed out of the way and crashed into someone else? Our thoughts can affect how we feel and behave.

This worksheet contains some common thinking errors related to anxiety and panic. For each thinking error, describe an example of one of your thoughts that falls into that category. Examples are provided.

| Thinking Error | Your Thought |
|---|---|
| Overestimating the probability of risk<br>E.g., "If I panic while driving, I will get in an accident." | |
| Overestimating the severity of the outcome<br>E.g., "My chest pain means I'm having a heart attack." | |
| Underestimating your ability to cope<br>E.g., "If I faint in the middle of class, I won't be able to handle it." | |
| Mind reading (believing you know what others are thinking about you)<br>E.g., "She won't want to date me if she knows I have panic attacks." | |

CONTINUED ▶

| Thinking Error | Your Thought |
|---|---|
| Emotional reasoning (using your feelings to judge reality, confusing your feelings and your thoughts) E.g., "I feel scared, so something bad must be coming." | |
| "Should" statements E.g., "I shouldn't feel anxious doing my job." | |

Describe how these kinds of thoughts have affected your panic:

_____

_____

_____

_____

_____

_____

_____

_____

_____

_____

_____

_____

# NOTICING YOUR THINKING ERRORS

One can get trapped in a spiral of negative thoughts. Following those thoughts down the rabbit hole fans the flames of your panic. Now that you have been practicing awareness of your thoughts, you can better recognize your thinking errors in the moment.

This week and beyond, notice these thoughts as they come up and label the type of error. For example, if you notice your arm is numb when you wake up and think, *I'm having a stroke*, recognize that you are overestimating the seriousness of this sign or the probability that something terrible is happening.

Spending a moment to do this can help you take a step away from your thoughts. Getting this extra space in your mind can allow you to pause and choose how you respond to these thoughts instead of becoming a victim of them.

From here on, treat your thoughts as guesses. Some may be completely accurate, but some may not. Recognizing that can help you challenge any skewed perceptions to handle your emotions in a more balanced, healthy way—and remind yourself that these thoughts are normal. Everyone has negative, automatic thoughts. They don't have to define who you are if you can learn to respond to them in a different way.

Describe how it feels to step away from your thoughts and label them:

_____

_____

_____

_____

_____

_____

_____

_____

_____

_____

# EVALUATE THE EVIDENCE

A helpful way of responding to your thoughts is to evaluate the evidence, which this exercise will give you an opportunity to try out. Evidence is not other thoughts, your feelings, or possibly even past patterns unless they are directly relevant to your current thought. Evidence is a concrete fact that would hold up in a court of law.

When you are evaluating the evidence, make sure to use the thought in its simplest form. For example, it would be difficult to evaluate the evidence for "I am going to make a mistake at work and lose my job and get evicted because I can't pay rent." But evaluating the evidence for "I am going to make a mistake at work" is a lot more manageable. Here's an example to get you going:

**Thought:** *She won't date me if she knows I have panic attacks.*

| Evidence For | Evidence Against |
|---|---|
| *None* | *I know she wants to date me because she told me she likes me.* <br> *I can't read her mind.* <br> *I can't predict the future.* <br> *She said she struggles with anxiety sometimes, so that shows she understands some of my struggle.* |

Now it's your turn:

Thought: _____

| Evidence For | Evidence Against |
|---|---|
|  |  |

| Evidence For | Evidence Against |
|---|---|
| | |
| | |
| | |

How do you feel now?

_____

_____

_____

_____

_____

_____

# "WHAT IF" THOUGHTS

Worries are any thoughts we have about possible negative experiences in the future. They often take form of "what if?" thoughts. For example, "What if the plane crashes?" or "What if I have a panic attack in the middle of class?" We can get stuck in a "what if" thought.

To manage your anxiety and panic in a healthy way, flip the "what if" around to a statement. Change "What if I have a panic attack in the middle of class?" to "I will have a panic attack in the middle of class." That gives you the opportunity to really understand your worry. Then evaluate the evidence for that thought as you did in the previous exercise. And ask yourself, "If that outcome really happened, how would I deal with it?" If you panicked in the middle of class, what then? Would no one help you? Would you be allowed to make up the assignment later? Would you be able to explain the situation to your teacher or your classmates?

Remember, the point is not to go down a rabbit hole of "what if" thoughts. Weigh the evidence and determine how you would cope for any "what if" thoughts that you have evidence for *in the present moment*. If the thoughts are about a completely imagined future, such as "What if I have a heart attack?" despite doctors saying you have no heart issues, engaging with the worry just activates your nervous system needlessly.

Mindfully notice the "what if" thought and then choose not to engage with it any further. You don't have to analyze it. You don't have to pay attention to it. This can be like the ticking of a clock. You can fixate on that ticking and it will quickly make you anxious or frustrated. Or you can notice the ticking in the background and continue about your day. Practice this new mindful way of responding to your worries every day this week.

Are any "what if" thoughts on your mind right now? Write the thought down here, rephrase it as a statement, and then evaluate the evidence. If you notice that this is a worry about a completely imagined future, write the thought down and then move on to the next section.

_____

_____

_____

_____

# REFRAME YOUR THOUGHTS

You've learned to recognize your thinking errors, evaluate the evidence for them, spot unhelpful worries, and identify how you would cope. What are you supposed to do once you've realized your thoughts are distorted? The final step is to develop a more realistic, helpful thought.

This is not necessarily "positive thinking." An unrealistic positive thought can be just as unhelpful as a distorted negative thought. The goal here is to come up with a realistic thought based on facts you can believe that would help you cope with the situation better. Aim to develop a thought that, if you rated it on a scale of believability from one to ten, you would rate it at least an eight.

Remember, your *interpretation* of something can be what is triggering or worsening your panic. Responding to yourself with a more rational, balanced thought can reduce your panic. Here's an example to illustrate the process you will soon have a chance to try yourself:

**Thought:** I am having a heart attack.

*Rate Your Emotions:*
**Panic:**

| 1 | 2 | 3 | 4 | 5 | 6 | 7 | (8) | 9 | 10 |

**Embarrassment:**

| 1 | 2 | 3 | 4 | 5 | 6 | (7) | 8 | 9 | 10 |

**Alternative Thought:** I have gotten an evaluation from my doctor that says my heart is healthy. Panic attacks do not lead to heart attacks.

**How much do you believe it?**

| 1 | 2 | 3 | 4 | 5 | 6 | 7 | (8) | 9 | 10 |

*Now That You've Reflected On Them Rate Your Emotions Again:*
**Panic:**

| 1 | (2) | 3 | 4 | 5 | 6 | 7 | 8 | 9 | 10 |

**Embarrassment:**

| (1) | 2 | 3 | 4 | 5 | 6 | 7 | 8 | 9 | 10 |

**Hope:**

| 1 | 2 | 3 | (4) | 5 | 6 | 7 | 8 | 9 | 10 |

CONTINUED ▸

Now you try it:

**Thought:** _____

_____

*Rate Your Emotions:*
**Panic:**

| 1 | 2 | 3 | 4 | 5 | 6 | 7 | 8 | 9 | 10 |

**Emotion:** _____

| 1 | 2 | 3 | 4 | 5 | 6 | 7 | 8 | 9 | 10 |

**Alternative Thought:** _____

_____

**How much do you believe it?**

| 1 | 2 | 3 | 4 | 5 | 6 | 7 | 8 | 9 | 10 |

*Now That You've Reflected On Them Rate Your Emotions Again:*
**Panic:**

| 1 | 2 | 3 | 4 | 5 | 6 | 7 | 8 | 9 | 10 |

**Previous Emotion:** _____

| 1 | 2 | 3 | 4 | 5 | 6 | 7 | 8 | 9 | 10 |

**New Emotion:** _____

| 1 | 2 | 3 | 4 | 5 | 6 | 7 | 8 | 9 | 10 |

## PRACTICING YOUR NEW THOUGHTS

This week, spot thinking errors that make you feel more anxious or panicked and then reframe them with alternative balanced thoughts. Write these thoughts down and keep them somewhere visible. Repeat the helpful thought to yourself as often as you can.

Remember, you are not telling yourself to stop thinking negative thoughts, because that won't help. When you notice a thinking error, acknowledge the thought and respond with your new realistic thought.

## THE FUNCTION OF WORRY

The reason we worry is so we can make an effective plan for any real threats. Worry without an effective plan is just activating your nervous system needlessly. If you have identified a real threat, make a plan and follow through with it. For example, if you worry that your symptoms are a sign of some serious illness, go to the doctor. If the doctor told you you're perfectly healthy, don't allow worry about your health to take over your life; focus on something else.

In this worksheet, identify one fear that is a valid, potential threat. Then create a plan for how you will address it. Next, decide what else you want to focus on.

| Worry ➡ | Plan ➡ | Focus |
| --- | --- | --- |
| | | |

CONTINUED ▸

Of course, part of an effective plan is also acknowledging what you *can't* control. Plan for what you can control and have evidence for, and let go of what you can't. You know that you can't just tell yourself to stop worrying. In this case, here are some things you can do to redirect your worries:

**Engage your attention in something you care about.** Distraction is unhelpful if you're afraid of the thoughts themselves or avoiding the feelings of anxiety or panic. But if you can recognize the thoughts and feelings aren't dangerous, you can choose to direct your mind away from your worry. When a worry comes up, don't push it away; acknowledge it as just a thought, and focus back on the things you want to be doing in the present moment.

**Schedule a worry date.** Delaying the thought until a later time can make you worry less. You may even forget about the things you were so worried about. So set up a worry date. Give yourself twenty minutes a day to worry. During that time, put in all the effort you can to focus on those worries. Get intense, and let all those worries in! If it's not your worry time, notice the worry and tell yourself to come back to it during your worry date.

**Meditate.** Meditation, as discussed, can help you be more aware and less judgmental of your thoughts. It also helps improve your ability to shift your attention at will.

*Thoughts are just thoughts. They are not who I am and do not have to control me.*

# Key Takeaways

Over this week, you have learned how thoughts can incite or reduce panic. Here are the key takeaways to keep in mind:

- What you think affects your emotions and behaviors. Sometimes our minds perceive something as threatening when it isn't. We all have automatic, negative, irrational thoughts. These may be random or may be shortcuts intended to protect us. If you misperceive something as dangerous, that can trigger your nervous system.

- Suppressing a thought causes a rebound effect. Mindfully observing your thoughts can reduce your worries and distressing symptoms.

- Distorted negative thoughts can lead to a cycle of escalating fear. While we are anxious or panicked, our thoughts become more negative to find the source of danger. That can lead to inflating worst-case scenarios or misinterpreting internal signals as serious signs of harm. Spotting your thinking errors can give you space to choose how to respond to these thoughts instead of becoming a victim of them.

- Weigh the evidence and determine how you would cope for any "what if" thoughts that you have evidence for *in the present moment*. If the thoughts are about a completely imagined future, mindfully notice the "what if" thought and then choose not to engage with it any further.

- Use all the information you gathered in evaluating your thoughts to come up with a realistic, helpful alternative. Any time that distorted thought comes up again, remind yourself it is normal, don't suppress it, and respond with your new helpful thought.

- Worrying without an effective plan activates your nervous system for no reason. If there are real dangers, plan for what you can control and let go of what you can't. Then redirect your attention away from that worry with the help of meditation, positive engagement in other things, or scheduling a worry date.

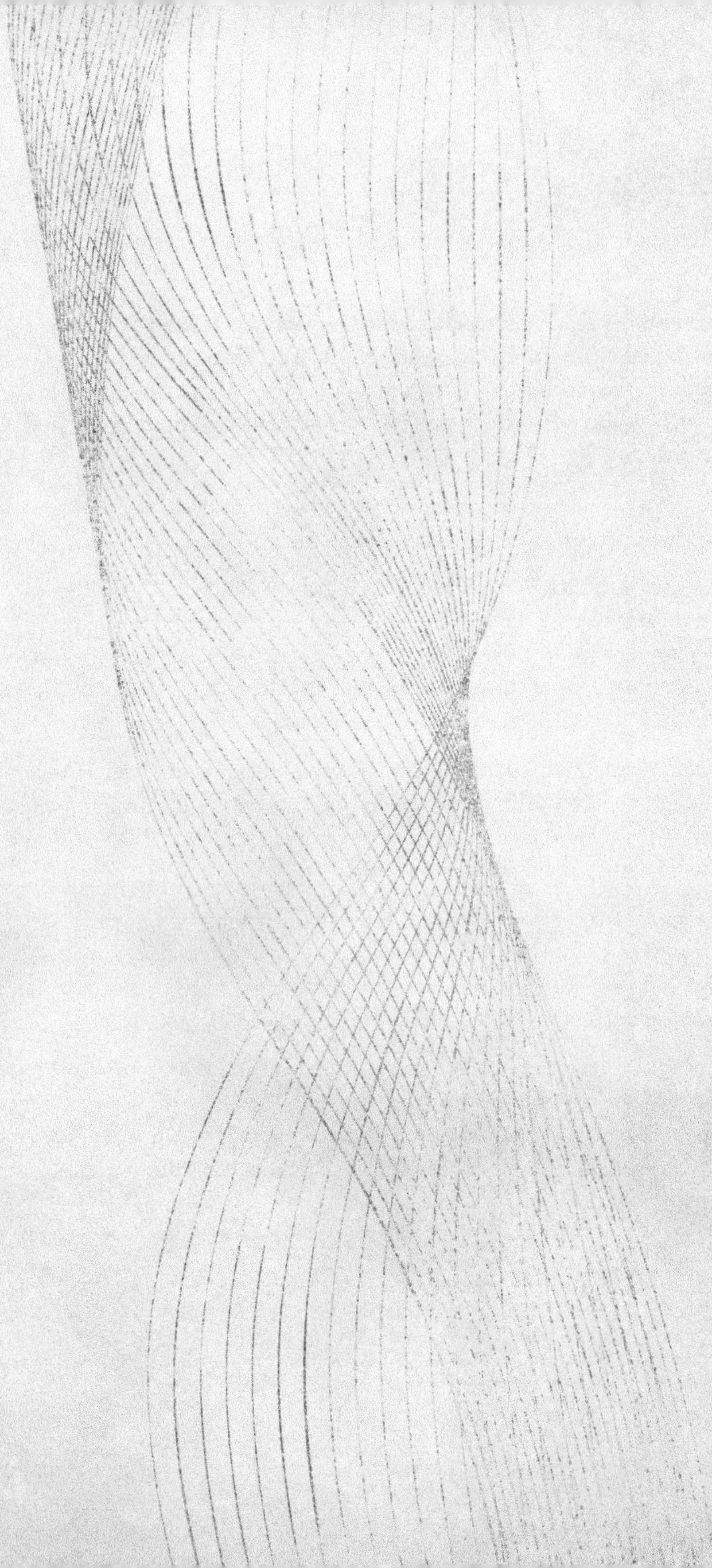

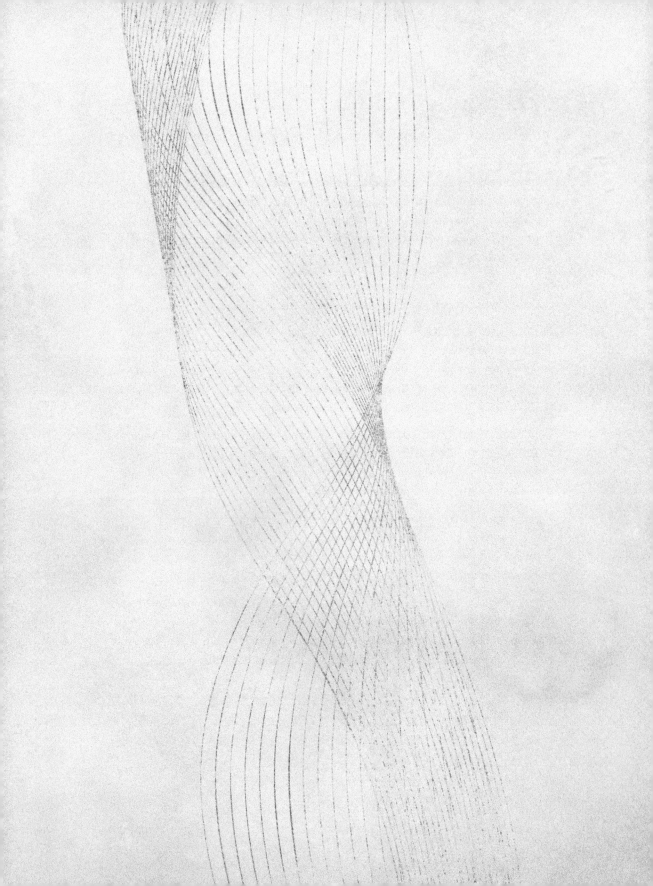

# Facing Your Fears

To truly overcome panic, you will need to confront it. By facing your fear, you can gain insight into your triggers and change the way your body responds to them. This week, you will engage in carefully designed exposure practices. Avoiding your triggers, as you've learned, reinforces fear. The goal of exposure is to teach your body and mind that fear is not necessary in situations that are, in reality, safe. Exposure, over time, can teach your nervous system to stand down, reducing the intensity of your symptoms. You may still have panic attacks, and you will still experience anxiety. But in changing the way you approach your panic, you can also learn that you are able to handle the feeling of fear and that it is not something you have to avoid.

Exposure *is* hard: Exposure practices require you to *feel* your anxiety or panic. You will literally be planning to be uncomfortable. Keep in mind that this discomfort can pay off in the long run by reducing your distressing symptoms. If you've never experienced exposure therapy, I recommend seeking out a mental health professional to support you. I also strongly encourage you to get an evaluation from a doctor before engaging in exposure to rule out possible medical causes for your symptoms and confirm it is safe to engage in your planned exposure practices.

Mia was sitting in her therapist's office. She felt hot and jittery, struggling to find a comfortable position in her chair. "How do I know my body won't just give out?"

Her therapist had just told her it was time for her to start the exposure part of treatment. Since starting therapy, Mia had been having fewer panic attacks and just generally feeling more confident in herself. But there were still things she avoided. For example, she hated the feeling of her heart pounding intensely. She knew it wasn't a heart attack and had various doctors give her a clean bill of health. But she dreaded what could happen. What if they were wrong? What if she had some mysterious condition no one caught? So, she wouldn't exercise and refused to participate in thrilling activities like roller-coaster rides.

She had learned that panic could not go on forever. But it was hard to believe that; when gripped by an attack, her body felt like it was turning against her.

"You don't know your body won't give out because you haven't given it the opportunity to try," her therapist said.

Mia grimaced, understanding the logic but still feeling panic begin to rise.

"Let's try a bit of exposure together. Can you do fifteen jumping jacks right now? Remember I'm here to support you, and if you look seriously hurt in any way, I'll call emergency services."

Mia trusted her therapist, but she didn't trust her body—and that was the issue. She took a few deep breaths and then began the exercise, feeling her panic skyrocket. But then she was on her eighth jumping jack, her ninth, her tenth, and although she felt uncomfortable, she realized her body was fine. Her heart rate was up, but she wasn't collapsing to the floor. She felt her panic subsiding.

# How Fear Escalates

As you've learned, your amygdala is monitoring your environment to detect any signs of danger and will activate your SNS when it does. To understand how fear escalates, you need to understand how the amygdala learns. The amygdala learns to trigger fear through *association*. Something does not have to be the cause of your fear to become a future trigger.

If your amygdala registers sensory information at the same time it registers something negative, any of that sensory information can become a trigger. That means if you were bitten by a dog, that dog itself can become a trigger for fear but so can the smells or sounds in the environment. If you were at a barbecue when this dog bit you, the smell of a barbecue can also become a trigger.

Your amygdala does not use words to communicate with you. Instead, it uses your physical sensations to convey that danger is present. You may feel a sudden sense of dread when encountering a trigger and possibly not even know why.

Fear can take two routes to initiate your SNS. It can originate in your cortex, where you are able to think about and evaluate a threat, and then be sent to your amygdala. This kind of anxiety can be alleviated through the thought-related skills you learned last week. But panic can take a shorter path designed to protect you in situations when even the milliseconds you would need to think may take too long for you to escape danger. It can skip your cortex and go straight to your amygdala.

In the shorter amygdala-originated path, you may be unable to rationalize yourself out of your fear and may not even be conscious of a trigger. If you are experiencing fear when you are logically telling yourself you know there is no danger, that's a good sign you are dealing with the shorter amygdala path of panic.

Fear becomes a cycle that feeds into itself due to your amygdala's reactions. If your amygdala has associated a harmless trigger with fear, it will incite that fear reaction over and over again when you encounter the trigger. In panic disorder, your brain has interpreted your own physical sensations as dangerous. Because we interpret fear as a sign of danger, this leads to avoidance, preventing your amygdala from learning any new associations to correct your mistaken fear response. Exposure is an incredibly powerful tool to help your amygdala develop new associations and ways of responding to your triggers.

# EXPLORING YOUR AMYGDALA'S ASSOCIATIONS

Your amygdala is constantly learning from your experience. Currently, your amygdala is creating an association between your triggers and your fear response. It looks like this:

**Trigger + Negative experience + Fear = Danger**

If we imagine the scenario of getting bitten by a dog, this is the association the amygdala has created:

**Dog + Bite + Fear = Danger**

Therefore, dog equals danger, leading the amygdala to activate the fear response whenever it encounters that trigger.

Here is an example of a possible negative association that could lead to panic disorder:

**Movie theater + Leaving abruptly, leading to embarrassment and the thought *People are judging me* + Panic attack = Danger**

Think about some of the difficult experiences you've gone through during your panic attacks that could have created this negative association. Try to identify the trigger and the negative experience that that led your amygdala to register it as dangerous.

# TEACH YOUR AMYGDALA

It is possible to teach your amygdala different associations by providing it with new experiences. You need to activate the same emotional response for your amygdala to be able to create new associations with the trigger. To change your amygdala's response, you need to experience your trigger and *actually feel the fear itself*. Specifically, you need to experience your trigger and fear response paired with a safe situation to teach your amygdala that it no longer needs to flare up fear to protect you.

These new memories can then contradict your original fear memory and open new, non-fearful responses. Exposure creates a new path your brain can take when presented with your trigger. Repeating the exposure and engaging with your trigger in different ways helps strengthen that new path:

**Trigger + Fear + Safe situation ≠ Danger**

If your trigger is a physical sensation itself, this is what that might look like:

**Heat beating fast + Fear + No heart attack ≠ Danger**

Exposure works by changing our expectations of danger. If we face the things we fear and nothing terrible happens, our brain learns that we don't need to be afraid. The situation doesn't have to be completely safe because we can tolerate reasonable risks. Repeated exposure lowers the fear response over time by providing your amygdala corrective experiences to make new, realistic associations with your trigger, as illustrated here:

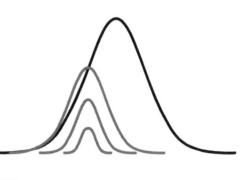

Now think of the triggers you identified earlier and some ways you can pair them with a safe situation, like in the previous example. Fill in the blanks.

**Trigger + Fear +** _____ *Safe Situation* _____ **≠ Danger**

**Trigger + Fear +** _____ **≠ Danger**

**Trigger + Fear +** _____ **≠ Danger**

# CREATE A FEAR HIERARCHY
# FOR SITUATIONS

Facing your trigger and realizing that your fear did not come true is a powerful way to teach your amygdala new associations. But even if you engage in exposure and the situation isn't completely safe, you can still learn new, positive things about it. If you face your fear and it turns out that people *did* judge you or the experience *was* uncomfortable, you can still gain insight into yourself. You may learn you are able to handle things you previously thought you couldn't. Or you may learn that the uncomfortable consequence doesn't matter as much as getting to do what you care about.

Now that you have a better understanding of how exposure can change your brain, it is time to start planning for it. To do so, you will create a fear hierarchy. Here's an example of how this might look:

*Situation Fear Hierarchy:*

**1. Getting on a plane alone**

1    2    3    4    5    6    7    8    (9)    10

**2. Public speaking**

1    2    3    4    5    6    7    (8)    9    10

**3. Taking public transit**

1    2    3    4    5    (6)    7    8    9    10

**4. Eating out alone**

1    2    3    4    (5)    6    7    8    9    10

To create your fear hierarchy, refer to "What Do You Avoid?" on page 49. Note each of the situations you avoid and rank each by the level of anxiety you would feel if you had to face it. Also, think about factors that would affect your anxiety level, such as length of time, being alone, or being far from home. And remember, you are only trying to reduce your fear response to things that are not actually harmful. If you are in real danger, you need your fear to protect you.

*Situation Fear Hierarchy:*

**1.** _____

1      2      3      4      5      6      7      8      9      10

**2.** _____

1      2      3      4      5      6      7      8      9      10

**3.** _____

1      2      3      4      5      6      7      8      9      10

**4.** _____

1      2      3      4      5      6      7      8      9      10

**5.** _____

1      2      3      4      5      6      7      8      9      10

**6.** _____

1      2      3      4      5      6      7      8      9      10

**7.** _____

1      2      3      4      5      6      7      8      9      10

# TEST YOUR EXPECTATIONS

To teach your amygdala new associations, you need to recognize your expectations about your triggers. Currently, you expect something bad will happen if you face your fear. You need to understand the specifics of that expectation to be able to test it, like a hypothesis. You can challenge some thoughts by weighing the facts you already have. But some thoughts, like the expectations you have about your fears, can only be challenged through direct experience. Exposure acts like an experiment for your hypothesis, helping you test the validity of your prediction and encourage new, realistic lessons about your fears.

In this activity, identify your expectations about the situations you avoid. Be as specific as possible. This helps you design exposure practices that aim to directly challenge those expectations. For example, if one of your expectations is that you'll feel bad, be specific about how (e.g., "My chest will hurt" or "I won't be able to sleep").

Think about the negative outcomes you fear and any related consequences. For example, if you expect other people to judge you, what do you fear about that? Do you worry that will make you feel bad, you won't be able to tolerate that bad feeling, or that the feeling will go on forever? Use the downward arrow technique on page 91 to get to the root of your feared expectation to help you with this exercise. Here are some examples:

| Situations You Avoid | Expectation |
|---|---|
| Getting on a plane alone | I will have a panic attack on the plane and won't be able to escape. If I can't escape, the panic will never end, and I could lose control. |
| Public speaking | If I make one mistake, I will have a panic attack and won't be able to handle the humiliation. |
| Taking the stairs | I will start to hyperventilate and pass out. |
| Exercising one hour from home | If my heart beats too fast, then I will have a heart attack. If I am too far from home, then I won't make it to the hospital. |

Now it's your turn:

| Situations You Avoid | Expectation |
|---|---|
| | |
| | |
| | |
| | |
| | |
| | |
| | |
| | |

# ENGAGING IN EXPOSURE

With the previous exercises under your belt, you are now prepared to engage in exposure. Exposure can either be done gradually or you can face your most intense fear all at once. Either method has been shown to be effective, but whichever method feels manageable is best for you.

Look over your situation fear hierarchy on page 128, and pick the situation that causes you a moderate level of fear, or the highest level of fear you can tolerate without having to escape or avoid your panic. Then come up with a deliberate way to confront the situation you have avoided, making sure to focus on your trigger and the actual outcome in the moment.

The goal is to engage in situations that directly test your expectations. You need to remain in the situation until you contradict that expectation. For example, if you are afraid you will faint due to hyperventilation if you go up more than three flights of stairs, plan to go up four flights of stairs to directly test and challenge that prediction. You are not trying to avoid feeling panic. You are trying to experience your panic without running away from your trigger to learn that the fear will naturally pass. This will be hard, and you will want to resist. Remind yourself that resistance is maintaining your fear. Lean into the feeling while using your skills to regulate your breath and respond to your thoughts in a more helpful way. Your fear may lower in the moment, but it does not have to for exposure to work.

Try to engage in exposure without relying on any relaxation tools so you can really teach your brain that the symptoms of panic are not scary. If you feel you may try to end or escape the exposure practice too early, you can use any of your coping skills to confront the situation, as long as you are not using them to avoid the experience. Remember, panic is uncomfortable but not dangerous.

Respond to the first two prompts *before* you practice exposure and then come back to answer the others after the practice:

What situation will you face this week?

_____

_____

_____

_____

What are you afraid will happen?

_____

_____

_____

_____

Did your fear come true? What really happened?

_____

_____

_____

_____

What did you learn?

_____

_____

_____

_____

# REPEAT THE PRACTICE

Engage in exposure for as long as you need or as many times as are necessary to disprove your prediction. Consider how the length of time and number of times the experience is repeated will affect your expectation. Some of your fears may be about long-term consequences. If you fear you will have a heart attack if you exercise too often, define what "too often" means to you (e.g., two times per week), and then engage in the situation at least once more than your feared prediction (e.g., three times per week).

This week, practice exposure as often as you can. Be consistent and deliberate. The more you practice, the faster you can get relief from your panic. At minimum, try to practice three times per week.

What is your exposure plan for this week?

_____

_____

_____

_____

_____

_____

_____

_____

_____

_____

_____

_____

_____

_____

# ELIMINATING SAFETY BEHAVIORS

As you have learned, safety behaviors reinforce your panic cycle. These behaviors prevent your amygdala from learning anything new about your triggers. Look back to the safety behaviors you identified on page 88.

Now that you have engaged in exposure, you can start to slowly remove your safety behaviors. For example, if your exposure plan was to ride the train for twenty minutes and your typical safety behavior is to talk on the phone to avoid your panic, plan to silence your phone. Choose items on your exposure list that would feel uncomfortable but not completely overwhelming. You *want* to activate your fear, but without becoming so overwhelmed that you run away.

If you feel an intense urge to leave the situation, use your coping card (see page 98) to lower the intensity of your symptoms to a manageable level, or take a break from the exposure for long enough to be able to return to it. Practice exposure while also removing a safety behavior at least once this week. Respond to the first prompt now; return to respond to the other after your practice.

What safety behavior will you stop using this week?

_____

_____

_____

_____

_____

What did you learn when you removed your safety behavior?

_____

_____

_____

_____

_____

# CREATE A FEAR HIERARCHY FOR PHYSICAL SENSATIONS

Exposure practices can also help your amygdala change its response to feared physical sensations. Exposure to physical sensations themselves is called interoceptive exposure. Review your responses to the "Measure Your Fear" exercise on page 95. Now, with those in mind, create a fear hierarchy for the physical sensations you fear or avoid. Here's an example:

## PHYSICAL SENSATION FEAR HIERARCHY

| Sensations You Avoid | Level of Anxiety/Panic (1–100) |
| --- | --- |
| Numbness/tingling | 95 |
| Shortness of breath | 80 |
| Heart pounding | 75 |
| Rise in body temperature | 65 |
| Sweat | 60 |
| Dizziness | 50 |
| Dry Mouth | 20 |

Now it's your turn:

## PHYSICAL SENSATION FEAR HIERARCHY

| Sensations You Avoid | Level of Anxiety/Panic (1–100) |
| --- | --- |
|  |  |
|  |  |
|  |  |
|  |  |
|  |  |

# PROVOKING YOUR SENSATIONS

Using the hierarchy that you created in the previous exercise, think of ways you can purposefully cause those sensations in order to expose your body to them. There's no need to try them yet. For now, just think about them. Here are some other ways to provoke various physical sensations:

| Physical Sensation | Ways to Trigger It |
| --- | --- |
| Hyperventilation | Breathe deeply, quickly, and forcefully. Breathe quickly through a straw. |
| Heart Pounding | Run. |
| Sweat | Turn up the heat. |
| Dizziness | Spin around in a circle. |
| Lightheadedness | Hang your head upside down, over the edge of the bed. |
| Derealization/Depersonalization | Stare in the mirror for a long period of time. Keep staring long enough to produce feelings of derealization or depersonalization. |

What else might you do to provoke these physical sensations?

_____

_____

_____

_____

# IDENTIFY EXPECTATIONS FOR PHYSICAL SENSATIONS

It is also helpful to identify expectations related to your feared physical sensations. List each physical sensation you want to avoid in the first column and then write what you fear will happen when you feel that symptom, such as having a stroke or losing your mind.

| Physical Sensations You Avoid | Expectation |
| --- | --- |
| | |
| | |
| | |
| | |
| | |
| | |
| | |

# PHYSICAL SENSATIONS EXPOSURE PRACTICE

With a clean bill of health from your doctor, it's time to engage in an exposure practice for a physical sensation. Facing your uncomfortable sensations directly instead of avoiding them teaches your amygdala that these sensations are not dangerous.

Now, similar to what you did for situations, engage in an exposure practice for a physical sensation. Allow yourself to feel that sensation for as long as or as many times as you need to disprove your expectation. For example, if you think feeling numb for more than one hour will cause neurological damage, sit on your leg for longer than one hour. You want to be able to stick with the sensation for enough time to gather relevant information about it. Don't just feel the sensation, but invite it in. Do this by saying something in your mind like "Bring on the panic. Make my heart pound and my body shake." This seems counterintuitive. But provoking your sensation with *willingness* and even humor will help your brain learn that it does not need to keep making you feel afraid to protect you from the sensation.

This week and beyond, engage in an exposure practice for your physical sensations as often as you can (at least three times per week). Remember, the lesson needs to be repeated over and over again for your amygdala to learn to respond in a new, productive way. Answer the following prompt now, and then return and answer the other prompts after you practice:

How will you engage in exposure to physical sensations this week?

_____

_____

Did your feared outcome happen?

_____

_____

Have any of your expectations changed? If so, why?

_____

_____

# INCORPORATING VARIETY FOR LONG-TERM PROGRESS

Here are some ways to make sure your progress lasts:

**Mix up the context.** The context in which you learn something can affect your ability to remember it. If you only engage in exposure with your therapist, you may only benefit from that lesson when you're with your therapist. To enhance your ability to retrieve your new lessons from exposure, mix up the context. Engage in exposure in different situations, with different people, at different times, with different amounts of time between each practice. This will improve your brain's ability to call up this new lesson instead of your old fear response.

**Mix up the order.** Traditionally, exposure was planned in the order of your level of distress, starting with the lowest level of fear and moving up the scale. New research indicates that varying the actual tasks of exposure can also improve your ability to recall your new way of responding. So instead of starting with less distressing tasks and moving up from there, switch it around a bit. For example, engage in exposure for something at level thirty, then jump up to level seventy, then back down to forty. A good strategy to follow is to engage in exposure in the order of what matters to you the most.

**Combine your triggers.** Engaging in exposure for not just one fear but two or more at a time can also deepen your learning. For example, you can plan to expose yourself to your fear of enclosed spaces and dizziness by going in the closet and spinning around.

With these ideas in mind, what are some ways you will add variety to your exposure plan?

_____

_____

_____

_____

_____

_____

# USING YOUR WORDS

Research, including a study published in *Psychological Science* in 2007, has shown that using language to process our experience activates a part of our brain that reduces activity in the amygdala. Labeling your experience while engaging in exposure can make it more manageable. Do this by labeling the emotions you are going through, in the moment and out loud.

When you notice your panic or anxiety during these exposure practices, you can also point out your amygdala's response—for example, "That's my amygdala telling me to be afraid." Then remind yourself you are teaching it something new.

Practice using your words for the next exposure you have planned.

*By facing my fears, I can change my brain to reduce my panic.*

## Key Takeaways

This week, you did what you probably thought was impossible. You faced your fears. You have done amazing work! Here are this week's main takeaways to support you in your continuing exposure practices:

- The amygdala learns to trigger fear through association. It may associate certain situations with fear or may register physical sensations themselves as threatening.

- Engaging in exposure to confront your feared situations or sensations can lower your fear response over time. Facing your triggers directly instead of avoiding them teaches your amygdala that they are not dangerous, and it does not need to keep making you feel afraid to protect you.

- Several important factors impact the success of exposure. You need to experience your trigger and fear paired with a generally safe situation to create new lessons about your trigger and your ability to tolerate reasonable risk. You need to purposefully disprove the expectations maintaining your fear.

- Make sure to focus on your trigger and the actual outcome in the moment to benefit from the experience. Safety behaviors reinforce fear, so slowly eliminate them as you confront your triggers.

- Engage in exposure for as long as or for as many times as are necessary to contradict your old expectations. Mix up the context and ways you engage in exposure to reinforce your new lessons. Combine your triggers in one exposure practice to deepen learning.

- You are not trying to avoid feeling panic. You are aiming to experience your panic without running away from your trigger to learn that the fear will naturally pass. Your fear does not have to reduce in the moment for it to lower in the long term.

- Try to engage in exposure without relying on any relaxation tools so you can really teach your brain that the symptoms of panic are not scary. But if you need to, you can use any of your coping skills to confront the situation, as long as you are not using them to avoid the experience. You can also take a break and then return to the exposure.

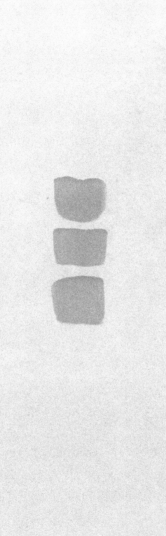

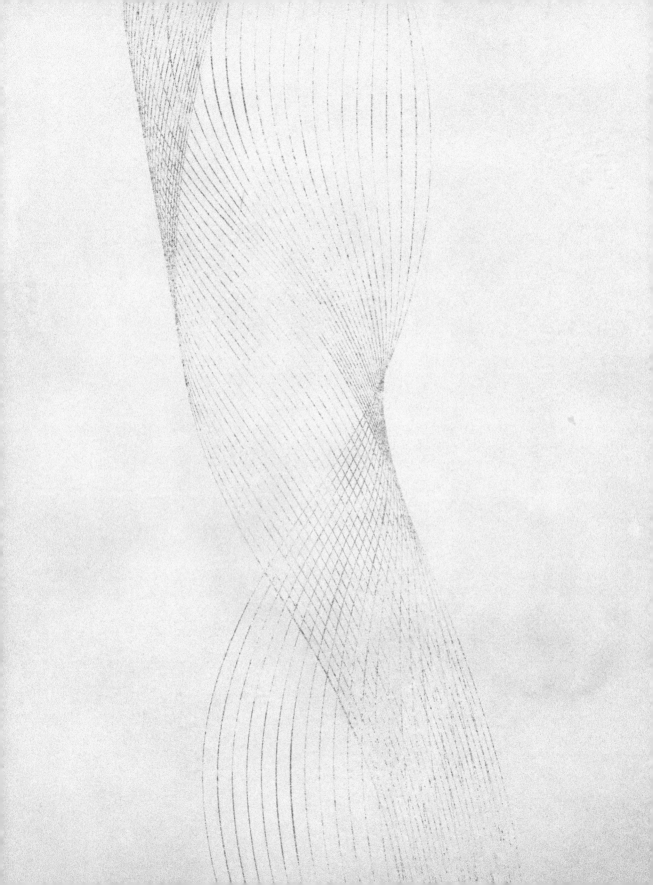

# Embracing the Moment with Mindfulness and Meditation

Mindfulness and meditation can relieve anxiety and improve the way you respond to stressors. A regular practice can help you be kinder to yourself and strengthen your ability to tolerate distress. This week, you will take a deeper dive into these practices. You will learn more about how to engage in meditation and develop your own regular practice. You will try out various forms of meditation and learn some tips to help you better understand and connect with meditative practices. You will explore any barriers that stand in the way of your practice and come up with steps to lower them. You will also learn how to engage in everyday mindfulness.

For each of the practices this week, read along with the script, record it to listen back to, or find similar meditations on meditation apps if you prefer. As you practice, remember to keep an open mind and be gentle with yourself.

Jack woke up in a panic. His sheets were drenched. His thoughts were racing. He felt crushed by a heavy sense of dread. He knew what might help, but meditating felt like the last thing he wanted to do right now. He also knew pretending this wasn't happening wouldn't make it go away. What's more, he had to get on a plane in a few hours. He did not need to be panicking right now.

Jack dragged himself out of bed, peeling the sheets away from his skin. Every part of his body felt extra sensitive. He settled into his armchair and took a deep breath. His breathing felt shallow, his chest constricted. He forced himself to take another breath. He tapped *begin* on his meditation app. As the voice guided him, he focused on just one breath—one inhale and then another.

He noticed his thoughts jangling around in his mind. And each time he got distracted by a thought, he took note of it and then brought his attention back to his breath. Jack was not trying to calm himself down, because he knew that forcing any feeling during meditation wouldn't help. He just noticed the sensations in his body and any thoughts as they darted in and out of his mind and continued to anchor his awareness in his breath.

As the minutes went on, he felt his heart rate slowing and his mind begin to quiet. The thunder of his panic started to recede. Without trying to make it so, he drifted into a familiar sense of ease. He felt lighter and less distraught. Jack opened his eyes, still feeling a little buzzy, but now ready to face his day.

# How Mindfulness and Meditation Can Help with Panic Attacks

Mindfulness originated from the practices of Buddhism. It became popular in the West in the 1960s and 1970s as more people traveled to Asian countries and brought the teachings home with them. *Mindfulness* is a way of relating to your experience (by being nonjudgmentally present and aware), and it can be done in informal everyday activities or as a formal practice. *Meditation* is a formal practice in which a technique, such as mindfulness, is used to foster awareness and equanimity.

There are many forms of meditation, including mindfulness meditation, mantra-based meditations, Transcendental Meditation, and loving-kindness meditation. Meditation is a rich practice you can spend years studying. There are also various therapeutic treatment modalities that use mindfulness as an intervention, including mindfulness-based stress reduction (MBSR), the Mindful Self-Compassion (MSC) program, and mindfulness-based cognitive therapy (MBCT).

For panic attack relief, you don't need to be a meditation expert to benefit from the practice. Various studies have shown that the use of mindfulness interventions can reduce rumination and symptoms of anxiety and improve mood and sleep. Your brain is neuroplastic, meaning that it can change. A common phrase in neuroscience is "neurons that fire together wire together." Your brain can be viewed like a garden. In a garden, the plants you tend to will grow, and what you don't cultivate will die off. Like nurtured plants in a garden, the neural circuits you use get strengthened. A variety of published research studies show that meditation can affect the structure of your brain, including strengthening the areas used for self-regulation and emotional, sensory, and cognitive processing.

When you experience panic, you are gripped by it, completely absorbed and taken over. Through the practice of mindfulness, you can learn to sit with your experience, observing your thoughts and sensations as they come up in a nonjudgmental way. This can give you a helpful pause, a moment to process what is happening in your body instead of immediately reacting.

# WHAT HAVE YOU EXPERIENCED?

Did you have any experience meditating before this workbook? Do you like it?
Find it useful? Does trying to meditate cause you more anxiety? Have you ever
practiced mindfulness? Describe your experience:

_____

_____

_____

_____

_____

_____

_____

_____

_____

_____

_____

_____

_____

_____

_____

_____

_____

_____

_____

_____

# MYTHS VERSUS TRUTHS QUIZ

Many people have mistaken beliefs about mindfulness and meditation that have gotten in the way of their ability to benefit from it or practice it at all. This activity will help you correct any myths you may believe. Mark each statement as myth or truth.

1.  **I need to clear my mind.** ............................................. Myth      Truth

2.  **During meditation, I will get distracted.** ............ Myth      Truth

3.  **Mindfulness can promote insight.** ...................... Myth      Truth

4.  **I am supposed to be relaxing.** ........................... Myth      Truth

5.  **Mindfulness can be practiced while meditating, but I can also be mindful of everyday experiences.** .......... Myth      Truth

6.  **I need to stop thinking.** .................................... Myth      Truth

7.  **I can't meditate if I'm anxious.** ...................... Myth      Truth

8.  **Mindfulness isn't about getting rid of thoughts but learning not to get caught up in them.** .............. Myth      Truth

9.  **I should be feeling good.** .................................. Myth      Truth

10. **Mindfulness is just focusing on my breath.** ........ Myth      Truth

11. **Non-striving, or being fully present without trying to change anything, is a core aspect of mindfulness.** ....... Myth      Truth

12. **Mindfulness involves awareness of any sensations, pleasant or unpleasant, without judgment.** .......... Myth      Truth

**ANSWER KEY**

**Myths:** *1, 4, 6, 7, 9, 10*

**Truths:** *2, 3, 5, 8, 11, 12*

Did any of the truths or myths surprise you? If so, why?

_____

_____

# TAKING A MINDFUL MOMENT

Instead of trying to clear your mind, prevent being distracted, or feel any specific way, I recommend you think about mindfulness like exercise. Imagine someone lifting weights. They will contract their muscle to lift the weight, and then release. The release is an inevitable and important part of the practice. You can't keep your muscle contracted forever. Each time you contract and then release your muscle, you are building strength and endurance.

Think about mindfulness in a similar way. Mindfulness is the exercise of contracting (focusing your attention) and releasing (becoming distracted) the muscle of your awareness. The more you practice, the better you get at being present and aware. It is important to remember that distraction is a natural part of the process. The moment you realize you are distracted *is* the practice of mindfulness. You then bring your attention back to the focus of the meditation. If you have to do this over and over again, that's fine. Each time you mindfully note your distraction and bring your attention back, that is building your ability to stay in the present moment.

Take a moment here to be mindful:

1. Set a timer for one minute.

2. Find something to focus on in the room you are in. This can be anything—from a piece of furniture to the pen on your desk. Now focus on that object.

3. Notice anything you can about it, such as the color, shape, and texture. Your mind will probably wander. When it does, notice that you have become distracted, and then bring your focus back to the object.

4. Concentrate your whole attention on this object, observing its different features. If you become distracted again, gently bring your attention back as many times as needed.

5. When the timer goes off, come back to reading this book.

# MINDFUL BREATHING MEDITATION

A meditation focusing on your breath can be a good place to start a mindfulness practice. Using what you learned in the previous exercise, practice this meditation a few times this week.

1.  Set a timer for five to ten minutes.

2.  Close your eyes and focus on your breathing.

3.  Notice the breath as it leaves your lungs. Then, as you inhale, focus on your lungs expanding.

4.  Keep your attention on the physical sensation of your breath. Focus on wherever you feel it strongest—from your nose to your chest to your stomach.

5.  If a thought distracts you, notice it. You can label it ("That's a thought"), but don't follow it. Bring your attention back to the breath.

6.  Follow the entire progression of your breath—from the inhale to the exhale to the next inhale.

7.  Now place a hand on your stomach and focus on the sensation of your belly rising and falling with the breath. Allow your breath to follow its natural rhythm. Don't try to control your breath. Simply rest your attention in it.

8.  You may have gotten distracted again by a thought or maybe a sensation. That's okay. Notice and label it, and then bring your focus back to the breath.

9.  When the timer goes off, bring your attention back to the room and open your eyes.

Describe your experience:

_____

_____

Does comparing mindfulness practice to exercising a muscle change anything for you?

_____

_____

Embracing the Moment with Mindfulness and Meditation    151

# USING MINDFULNESS AND MEDITATION FOR PANIC RELIEF

Here are some tips to make mindfulness and meditation part of your panic attack management plan:

- Develop a daily meditation practice. You get more benefit from it the more you do it.

- Try many different types of meditations. I view meditation like reading or television. There are so many options, and everyone has their personal preferences. For example, you may prefer visualization to focusing on your body. Allow yourself to explore different kinds of meditations to find one you connect with.

- If you like guided meditations, consider using an app. Meditation apps have lots of guided options.

- If you prefer to meditate with other people, sign up for a meditation group.

- Make your practice your own. There is no specific amount of time to meditate. If you only have one minute to meditate, that's okay.

- Practice mindfulness as often as you can. Mindfulness can be a form of meditation, but it can also be practiced anytime. It is simply moment-to-moment awareness of the present moment, including thoughts, sensations, and surroundings, without judgment. Practice being mindful during everyday activities, such as washing the dishes and eating.

- Learn from the experts. Consider taking a meditation course or reading a book on meditation. Meditation experts have a wealth of wisdom that can deepen your practice.

How will you incorporate mindfulness and meditation into your plan?

_____

_____

_____

_____

What, if any, barriers to practicing mindfulness or meditation still remain?

_____

_____

_____

_____

What types of support can help you with your practice? Would meditating with a friend keep you accountable? Do you need to set alarms for a reminder? Do you want to learn more about meditation before making it a regular habit? Describe the support that could be helpful:

_____

_____

_____

_____

_____

# MAKING SPACE FOR SOMETHING NEW

Every one of your coping tools serves some kind of function—even the unhealthy ones. They are all trying to help you survive. Your panic comes from your threat-defense system, but you have another system that can help you cope as well: your mammalian-care system. This is the system accessed when we feel the motivation to care for our loved ones or ourselves.

This practice and its related prompts are adapted from Kristin Neff's MSC program. It can help you make space for that system. Set aside five to ten minutes for this practice.

1. Close your eyes and think of a recent moment when you struggled with panic. Maybe it was during exposure therapy or a stressful event at school or work. Call up the details of this experience.

2. Bring up the words that surfaced in your mind. Allow yourself to remember even the harshest things you said to yourself. Face the words of your inner critic.

3. Focus on the physical sensations of panic at the time. Your heart pounding, your body tensing—whatever sensations came up.

4. Practice saying thank you, either out loud or in your mind. Thank your threat-defense system for all the ways it was trying to protect you. Send that part of yourself (the part that can get the most negative and defensive) gratitude. Thank your panic for doing all this work to make sure you survive.

5. Now ask it to move to the side. Tell it, "Thank you, but I also need space for something else." And ask it to make space for kindness, compassion, and support. Imagine an actual space being cleared inside of you. Imagine filling up that space with your care system.

6. Now allow yourself to feel whatever is coming up for as long as needed, and when you are ready, open your eyes.

How did it feel to send gratitude to a part of you that you've struggled so much with?

_____

_____

_____

How are you feeling now?

_____

_____

_____

_____

_____

What were the words you heard? What does your inner critic tell you when panic rises? Write those words here:

_____

_____

_____

_____

_____

Now close your eyes and think about the words you wished you heard. If you could hear the perfect words, imagine what they would be. When you are having the hardest time, think about what you would like someone to tell you to make it easier to bear. Write those words here:

_____

_____

_____

_____

_____

# LOVING-KINDNESS MEDITATION

A loving-kindness meditation involves sending yourself or others phrases of goodwill. Sending yourself goodwill can help when you are struggling with panic. There are many common phrases used during loving-kindness meditations, such as "May you be well" or "May I be kind to myself."

During this meditation, an adaptation of Kristin Neff's MSC program, you will use the goodwill phrases you came up with in the previous prompt.

1. Take a moment to ground yourself in your body by taking a couple deep breaths.

2. Now say your goodwill phrases aloud or in your mind. Really allow yourself to accept the words you need to hear. Notice how they make you feel.

3. Repeat the phrases. Earnestly send yourself these messages of support.

4. It's okay to get distracted. When you notice you are distracted, observe the thought or sensation, and allow it to leave without following it. Then gently bring your attention back to the phrases, sending them to yourself again.

5. Repeat them again, as many times as needed.

6. When you are ready, bring your attention back to the room, and open your eyes.

This week, use this loving-kindness meditation before or after each exposure practice to support yourself in the hard work you're doing.

*Everyone can meditate. The more I practice, the more it can help me.*

# MINDFULNESS PRACTICE
# FOR OVER-MONITORING

Awareness of your body is important, but over-monitoring and endlessly worrying about your body's sensations can quickly exacerbate your panic. For example, pay attention to your nose. Focus on any sensations that come up. Did you start to feel an itch, a tingle, or any new sensation you had not noticed before? We have all kinds of sensations in our bodies that we don't pay attention to. If we become hyper-focused on those sensations, we could worry needlessly.

Over-monitoring your body could be contributing to your cycle of panic. Practice being mindful of it. Notice when you are fixating on physical sensations in a mindful, nonjudgmental way such as "I am paying a lot of attention to my heartbeat." Then choose to move your attention to something you want to focus on.

This is not thought-stopping, but instead using the skill of mindfulness to notice when you are hyper-focusing on your body without criticism and choosing to redirect your attention. Instead of engaging with the worry about what a physical sensation may mean, notice the worry: "I am worrying about what my chest pain means."

Then, like a meditation, choose to focus on what you care about in the present moment instead of letting your panic or anxiety hold you back. Be gentle and compassionate as you do this. Don't berate yourself. Instead, note your worry and acknowledge, "This is hard for me right now, but I am going to choose to focus on what I want to." Practice this regularly.

# BASIC MINDFULNESS MEDITATION

You have now practiced meditation focusing on your breath and different aspects of your body. Through practice, you are getting a better feel for mindfulness itself. The breath is often used as an anchor during mindfulness because it's relatively easy to notice and it can be helpful to focus on just one thing. But you can spread your awareness past your breath or your body. This is a meditation you can use to practice that. Set aside about five minutes.

1. Take a deep breath. Notice the feeling of air coming into your lungs and then leaving.

2. Now become aware of anything that is happening in this moment. Allow your attention to rest in the present.

3. You may experience emotions, thoughts, or sensations. Notice your experience in this moment, without trying to change it.

4. If a thought comes up, don't resist it, but don't follow it. Just notice the thought and let it leave just as easily as it came.

5. You will get distracted. Notice that distraction. Don't criticize yourself or try to be anything other than what you are right now.

6. Allow an open awareness of your internal and external world.

7. If you notice your breath, allow yourself to be with the breath; notice your inhale and your exhale. Don't try to control your breathing. Just let it be.

8. If you notice a feeling, allow that feeling. Don't push it away. Just mindfully experience it.

9. You may notice the sensation of your body against the chair, the sounds around you, or scents in the air. Let yourself be with anything that is coming up right now, without judgment.

10. When you are ready, take one last deep breath to finish this meditation.

Practice this meditation at least once this week.

Did any sensations of panic or anxiety come up?

_____

_____

_____

_____

If you felt any uncomfortable feelings, what was it like to notice them in a mindful, nonjudgmental way?

_____

_____

_____

_____

How do you feel now?

_____

_____

_____

_____

# EVERYDAY MINDFULNESS

Mindfulness is not just something you do when sitting in place. Plan for a time where you can set aside ten to fifteen minutes without interruption for mindful movement.

1. Go for a walk, either in your own neighborhood or in a place where you can feel comfortable and are able to take in your surroundings. If mobility is an issue, take a scenic drive instead.

2. Leave the earbuds out, and instead mindfully notice anything around you. Notice the colors of the plants and flowers. Notice the feel of your feet making contact with the ground. Notice any noises, such as people or birds.

3. Mindfully experience your body as it moves. Focus on the sensation of your breath as you take each step or the lurch of your body as you turn. Really engage all your senses.

4. Distraction will be a natural part of this. When you become distracted, gently bring your awareness back to the present moment.

5. Continue to do this for the length of your walk.

To get in the habit of practicing everyday mindfulness this week and beyond, do this practice at least once a week.

# SET UP YOUR MINDFULNESS AND MEDITATION CALENDAR

Now that you have learned several different ways to practice mindfulness and meditation, plan to engage in one practice each day. Use this calendar to plan out your practice. Here's an example:

| Monday | Tuesday | Wednesday | Thursday | Friday | Saturday | Sunday |
|---|---|---|---|---|---|---|
| *Mindful walking* | *Body scan* | *Progressive muscle relaxation* | *Mindful eating* | *Mindful breath meditation* | *Loving-kindness meditation* | *Basic mindfulness* |

| Monday | Tuesday | Wednesday | Thursday | Friday | Saturday | Sunday |
|---|---|---|---|---|---|---|
| | | | | | | |

After a week of mindfulness and meditation activities, how do you feel?

_____

_____

_____

_____

## LET'S REVIEW

What have you learned about mindfulness and meditation?

_____

_____

_____

_____

How do you feel about mindfulness and meditation now?

_____

_____

_____

_____

Which practices will you use in your daily life?

_____

_____

_____

_____

*Meditation can reduce my stress and increase my awareness.*

# Key Takeaways

This week, you became a meditation practitioner! You learned about mindfulness and tried out several kinds of meditations. Here are the key takeaways:

- Mindfulness and meditation can reduce anxiety, increase your awareness, and improve your mood, ability to tolerate stress, and sleep. It can affect the structure of your brain in positive ways.

- Mindfulness is moment-to-moment awareness of any part of your experience in a nonjudgmental way. Mindfulness can be a form of meditation. But it can also be practiced outside of meditation. Practice being mindful during everyday activities.

- Being fully present without trying to change anything is a core aspect of mindfulness. Mindfulness isn't aiming to get rid of your thoughts; rather, it is learning to not get caught up in them.

- Mindfulness is the exercise of contracting (focusing your attention) and releasing (becoming distracted) the muscle of your awareness. The more you practice, the better you get at being present and aware. Distraction is a natural part of the process. The moment you realize you are distracted *is* the practice of mindfulness. Then you bring your attention back to the present.

- A regular meditation practice can help you respond in a more productive way to panic. Develop a daily meditation practice as part of your panic attack management plan.

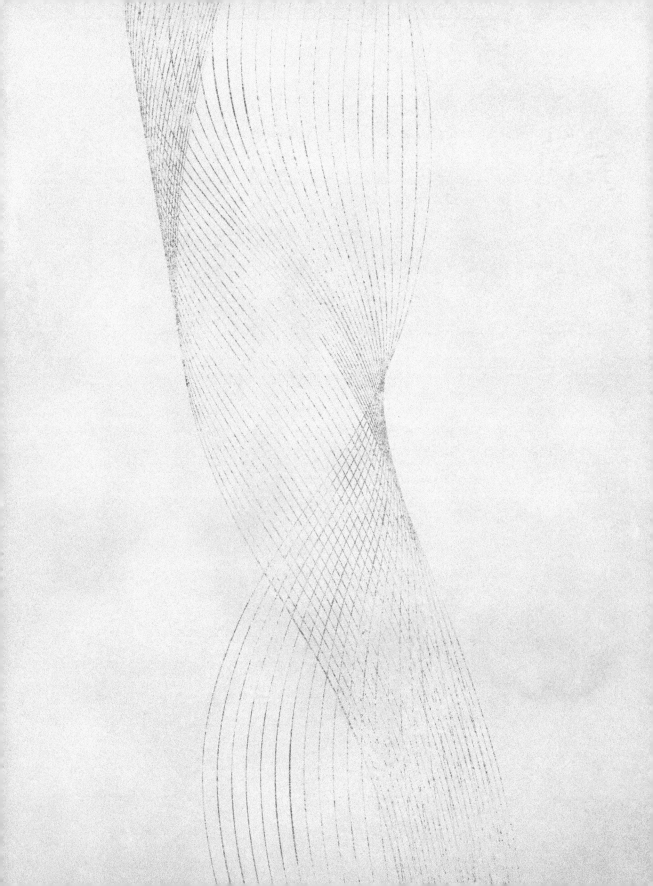

# Bringing All the Pieces Together

You have been developing a complex understanding of your body, thoughts, and behaviors. You have learned skills to target the different aspects of your panic. This week, it's time to bring together everything you've learned to ensure you have a well-rounded plan for your future.

This week, you will follow a step-by-step guide for combining the skills and tools you've learned. You will review your progress and identify your continuing challenges to address future roadblocks. You will reflect on what your panic looks like now and how your views of yourself have changed. Then you will practice putting it all together. You will learn tips to maintain your progress, including exploring your social circle and identifying people or resources you can turn to for support. You will define goals for the future so you can keep building on this plan.

Antonia had been on the treadmill for thirty minutes. She had learned that aerobic exercise was helpful in managing her panic. She stepped off, distracted by her plans for dinner. Suddenly, she realized she was becoming more anxious and began to feel faint. She noticed her heart pounding, her palms sweating, and tingling in her calves and feet. Her eyes scanned the room as her fear mounted. Her thoughts started to race: "What am I missing? What's wrong?" Her stomach clenched, and the feeling of panic hit her.

Antonia took a deep breath and began to focus on her body. She labeled the changes that had caused her rising panic. She recognized that she had just been running, which caused her pounding heart and sweaty palms. She also remembered that she had stepped off the treadmill without a cooldown period because she'd been distracted. This was likely the cause of her lightheadedness and tingling sensations. She realized she had been searching the room for the source of her fear and remembered that she previously learned her mind would shift into a state of threat detection when experiencing panic.

She began feeling calmer, understanding that there was no actual threat and that her body had misinterpreted unrelated symptoms as cues to panic. Her heartbeat slowed, her body began to cool down, and her thoughts settled. Antonia stopped a panic attack in its tracks, using the tools and insights she had learned.

# Review and Reflect on Your Progress

We tend to pay more attention to our setbacks than our successes. But feeling like we are making progress in meaningful work is what motivates us to keep doing that work. A sense of progress also helps us manage the tough feelings that will inevitably come up. Recognizing your success moves you forward. The best way to harness your progress is to actively notice your small wins. Every small win builds momentum for later success. We need to believe in our ability to affect things in our lives in order to be motivated to do the work of change. This week, you will highlight the progress you've made to motivate you to make this seven-week plan into a lifestyle change. Be sure to keep tracking your progress so you can sustain this plan into your future.

Also remember, this plan is meant to fit *your* needs. An important part of reflecting on it is assessing what isn't working. Your struggles don't have to hold you back. This week, you will review what has worked and pay attention to what hasn't. Recognizing your challenges helps you learn from them so you can continue to make progress.

Understanding how to apply your plan to specific aspects of your panic or specific situations will help you feel ownership of this plan. It will help you feel confident to handle the challenges that come, even the new or unpredictable ones. The whole point of these last few weeks has been to help you learn that you can't control your emotions, but you *can* feel capable of managing them.

## DEVELOPING YOUR COMPREHENSIVE PLAN

Here is a step-by-step plan to bring all your skills together:

1. Engage in exposure for any fears you know will not hurt you. Remember that key aspects of exposure include disproving your expectations and varying how you engage in exposure to deepen your learning. Be consistent, deliberate, and repetitive with this practice. If you notice old fears creeping up, return to engaging in exposure to reinforce your new realistic learning. Also, work on eliminating safety behaviors to show your brain you don't need to be afraid of your triggers.

2. Practice awareness of your body and label your emotions. Practice observing your physical and emotional experience without judgment, but do not over-monitor and engage in excessive worry about your body. You are focusing on learning that anxiety and panic can be uncomfortable, but that discomfort is not dangerous. Practice nonjudgmental acceptance of your inner experience as often as you can.

3. Engage in activities that lower your overall level of stress, like meditation and exercise. But don't use them as safety behaviors to avoid anxiety.

4. Recognize your thoughts and evaluate the evidence for them. Being able to identify when your thoughts have become distorted will help you respond to them in healthier ways. Mindfully notice unhelpful worries based on imaginary scenarios you don't have evidence for in the present moment. Redirect your attention away

CONTINUED ▶

from worries that are not concrete problems right now. Instead, focus on what you care about in the present.

5. Come up with helpful, realistic thoughts to say to yourself or keep posted somewhere visible. Repeat these helpful thoughts as often as needed. Remember, repetition is an important part of learning.

6. Use what you care about to motivate yourself to keep doing what you need to do to manage your panic.

Describe the next steps you will take to manage your panic:

_____

_____

_____

_____

_____

_____

_____

_____

_____

_____

_____

_____

_____

_____

_____

_____

_____

# PLANNING EXPOSURE IN INCREMENTAL STEPS

Don't beat yourself up if you haven't been able to face some of your fears. Your fear is very convincing. It's supposed to be. It's why we have survived as a species.

Don't give up, either. Instead, plan exposure in incremental steps. For example, if you are afraid of hyperventilating and can't provoke the sensation for longer than a minute, start with thirty seconds. If you are afraid of driving and can't quite get yourself to start the car, then just sit in it for a while, allowing yourself to feel the anxiety in that moment. You can scale any exposure practices down to the smaller steps you are ready to face to help you build up to your scariest triggers.

There is also a type of exposure that just uses your imagination. It's called imaginal exposure. If you don't feel quite ready to face the situation or physical sensation in real life, write out a script of what you're afraid of. Include all the details you can, including what you would feel, your thoughts, and your actions. Record yourself reading the script and play it back, actively imagining yourself in the situation.

How did your imaginal exposure go? What came up for you?

_____

_____

_____

_____

What, if anything, did you learn from that experience?

_____

_____

_____

_____

# LET'S REFLECT

Think back to your goals in the beginning. What progress have you made?

_____

_____

_____

_____

_____

Describe some of your big or small successes:

_____

_____

_____

_____

_____

No one is perfect and no panic attack management plan will be, either. Now that you've really put the work in to learn about your panic and confront your fears, some things may have improved but you may still be struggling in some areas. In what ways are you still struggling with panic?

_____

_____

_____

_____

_____

# ADDRESS FUTURE ROADBLOCKS

Brainstorm some ways you can address your ongoing struggles. Think about the things you've learned, and also think about outside resources you could rely on to help you with these challenges. For each ongoing struggle you identify here, describe your ideas to get help so it doesn't block your path ahead in the future.

| Ongoing Struggles | Ideas to Help |
| --- | --- |
| | |
| | |
| | |
| | |
| | |
| | |

*Challenges are not failures. They are opportunities to learn and grow.*

# PUT IT ALL TOGETHER

This week, did you have a panic attack or struggle with anxiety? Think about a specific moment you found difficult recently. Remember that your thoughts, feelings, and behaviors can all affect each other. Understanding that connection can help you put all your skills together to effectively deal with your panic. Now describe the aspects of your recent struggle in terms of your thoughts, feelings, and behaviors. Write them in the corresponding areas in the diagram.

Now think about what you could have done to deal with your panic in a healthy way (or what you already did). Fill in the tools you used or could use in the future to address each aspect of your panic:

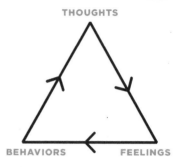

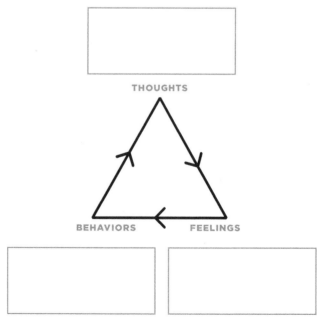

# PUTTING IT INTO PRACTICE

Use everything you've learned in your everyday life. When you feel anxiety or panic coming on, think back to the connection between your thoughts, feelings, and behaviors. Break your experience into those three aspects to better understand what's going on. Then actively use the strategies that you know work for you to address each aspect of your panic or anxiety.

Remember, managing your panic will be a constant work in progress. Some days will be easier than others. Change is not linear. You might have days when you feel like you're backsliding. That doesn't mean you've thrown all your progress out the window. That just means you're human.

When you stumble, ask yourself what you can learn from the experience. And make sure to engage in regular self-care. Managing your panic isn't just about what you do in the moment but also about keeping your stress levels down by taking care of your body and mind on a consistent basis.

What are your expectations of panic now?

_____

_____

_____

_____

_____

Now that you've almost completed this workbook, how do you view yourself?

_____

_____

_____

_____

_____

CONTINUED▸

How has panic or anxiety changed in the different areas of your life? Describe those changes in each area:

**Relationships:**

_____

_____

_____

_____

**Work/School:**

_____

_____

_____

_____

**Health/Physical:**

_____

_____

_____

_____

**Daily Activities:**

_____

_____

_____

_____

# IDENTIFY YOUR SUPPORT SYSTEM

No one has to manage panic on their own—and no one should. As you prepare yourself to continue tackling panic in the long term, it is a good idea to assess your support system. Here are some helpful questions:

- Who can you turn to when you feel the worst, when your urge to run away and hide from it all gets overwhelming?

- Who can you involve in your exposure plans, especially when you first start facing your fears?

- Who will be your cheerleader?

In the following diagram, fill in the names of the people who make up your social life, as follows:

1. In your *inner circle*, fill in those people you feel closest to. These are the people you trust and can go to for almost anything. This may include your partner, your family, your closest friends, or mentors.

2. Then, in the next circle, fill in the people you *share important experiences* with. They may be friends, coworkers, or classmates. These are people who support you but possibly not in all the areas of your life.

3. Then, in the outside circle, fill in your *acquaintances*. This may include people you are casually friendly with, neighbors you might chat with, or any new relationships.

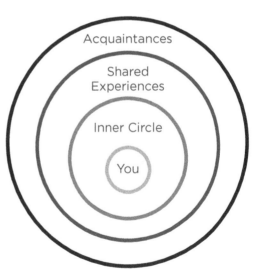

CONTINUED▸

Who will you include in your panic attack management plan?

_____

_____

_____

_____

How can the people in your life support you in dealing with your panic?

_____

_____

_____

_____

Are there any people you'd like to be closer to? If so, what can you do to deepen those relationships?

_____

_____

_____

_____

# TALKING ABOUT YOUR PANIC

Just as avoidance reinforces fear, so does hiding. Many people who suffer from panic attacks feel a lot of shame about it. We are still working on destigmatizing mental health issues, and most people aren't getting the appropriate education or having open conversations about panic and anxiety. But panic is natural and universal. You don't have to feel ashamed about experiencing something normal.

If you hide your panic, tell lies to prevent people from finding out about it, or pretend this is not something you're struggling with, you make panic the monster under the bed. Keeping your panic a secret maintains your belief that it *is* something to be embarrassed about or ashamed of. Opening up about it can help you reduce your panic symptoms. Talking about something so uncomfortable is hard. It's important to validate that, but if you practice, it can get easier.

This week, start talking about your panic with people you trust, those in your inner circle. Have conversations with those you know care about you and want to support you. Once you've gotten more comfortable with that, start sharing about it in more casual relationships. The more you can talk about your panic and anxiety as if it's a run-of-the-mill thing, the more you will realize that everyone struggles with these feelings and that you are not alone.

The more you normalize your panic, the less scary it will become. Just keep in mind that you want to talk about it with people who have shown you a good track record of understanding. If there is anyone in your life who has been cruel to you about your panic, they don't need to be the people who get the benefit of being involved in your wonderful work. But allow yourself to connect with those who can support you.

# MAINTAINING YOUR PROGRESS

Managing your panic is a lifelong journey. This workbook is structured in seven weeks to give you the most effective tools in a short amount of time so you can build on your own momentum. But panic attack management will not be over in seven weeks. To fully benefit from your plan, you have to keep taking care of your mental health. And you have to develop a plan to sustain your progress. Here are some helpful tips:

**Set up an accountability system.** That might involve alarms or reminders for you to practice your tools. You may want to schedule things like exposure or meditation in your calendar to make sure you follow through. Or you can ask someone to be your accountability buddy.

**Leverage social support.** You can join a support group or take a meditation class. It may be easier to maintain your progress if you have a solid group structure to keep you connected.

**Use outside tools.** There are so many apps, podcasts, and educational materials specifically designed for anxiety and panic. See the Resources on page 184 for suggestions, but don't feel limited to just those. Use what feels right to you; just confirm that the information comes from a reputable source. Sometimes mental health concepts get lost in translation in a short video or blog, so make sure your resources cite their sources or clearly identify their relevant credentials.

**Go to therapy.** This book can be used on its own or as a companion tool in therapy. If you are actively participating in the activities but still feel like you're struggling with panic, that's a good sign to contact a mental health professional. Or if these tools worked for you for a while but now you feel they don't, that's also a good time to reach out for help.

**Set aside time for you.** That doesn't mean time to watch TV or grab brunch with friends (although those are perfectly great activities). Actually set aside time to be alone with yourself to process and understand your thoughts and feelings. If you don't give yourself that personal time, mental health issues can creep up on you.

## WHAT ARE YOUR FUTURE GOALS?

Now that you're almost done with your seven-week plan, let's look to the future. What are your goals moving forward?

_____

_____

_____

_____

_____

_____

_____

_____

## PAYING IT FORWARD

You have learned a lot about panic, but you are not a mental health expert. Nevertheless, teaching can give you a deeper and longer-lasting understanding of new information. So, a great way to cement what you've learned about panic is to teach others about it.

Again, it's important to avoid being an armchair therapist. If someone in your life needs the help of a mental health professional, encourage them to seek out therapy for themselves. But if you know some tool or piece of information that could be helpful, go ahead and share it.

We all benefit from mental health care when we pass along effective and evidence-backed lessons. And every time you teach something about panic, you make the lesson stronger for yourself. This week, teach someone one thing you learned about panic—and then keep spreading the knowledge.

Mistakes are a natural and inevitable part of this process. Give yourself grace. Remember to be kind and flexible with yourself. Being overly critical is not going to reduce your panic. In fact, it will probably make it worse. Self-compassion is necessary for panic attack relief. Be compassionate with yourself as often as you can.

There is no such thing as failure in this plan, just lessons to learn from moments you feel stuck. Sometimes the lesson will be acknowledging that a particular tool or strategy just isn't the right fit for you. And, at other times, the lesson will point to outside support you need. That's okay. Be curious and treat yourself the way you would treat a close friend going through a hard time.

*Panic is not a mysterious monster. Panic is a normal emotion I now know how to manage.*

## Key Takeaways

You just reached the end of this workbook. That's amazing! Your panic attack management plan is off to a great start. Here are important takeaways for your future:

- Recognize your small wins as often as you can. Feeling like you are making progress in meaningful work will increase your self-confidence and motivate you to keep doing the work.

- Continue to actively identify where you struggle. When you experience a setback, ask yourself what you can learn from the experience. Be honest with yourself about what's not working or reach out for support when you need it.

- Remember the connection between your thoughts, feelings, and behaviors. Break your experience into those three aspects to better understand what's going on and what strategies you need to use to address each aspect of your panic or anxiety.

- You can scale any exposure practices down to the smaller steps you are ready to face to help you build up to your scariest triggers. Focus on learning that anxiety and panic can be uncomfortable, but that discomfort is not dangerous.

- Engage in regular self-care. Managing your panic isn't just about what you do in the moment but also about proactively taking care of yourself.

- Outside support is an important part of managing your panic. Open up to people about your panic or teach them what you've learned to maintain your progress. The more you connect with others about your panic or anxiety, the less scary it will become.

- Managing your panic is a constant work in progress. You will struggle and make mistakes. That's a normal part of the process.

- Remember to be kind and flexible with yourself. You can't control your emotions, but you can use the tools you've learned and insights you've developed to manage them in a healthy way. And remember, the best way to benefit from this plan is to continue putting it into practice in the long term.

*To keep up my progress, I will use all my new skills and insights regularly and consistently.*

# A FINAL NOTE

You have done incredible work. Over these last seven weeks, you have been brave, vulnerable, and willing to learn. You have faced your fears and put in hard work to change your brain for the better. You should be proud of yourself, so take a moment here to celebrate.

As you change your relationship to panic, your life will feel freer, lighter, and more connected. Enjoy that. Let yourself pause and relish the changes. Allow yourself to take new risks and go after whatever panic used to stand in the way of. And give yourself credit for your wonderful accomplishment.

If you're still struggling, that's okay. Remember that perfection isn't the goal. Finding your way to a life you can enjoy living is. This workbook is structured in seven weeks, but that's more of a suggestion than a rule. Go at your own pace. Review any parts of this workbook as often as needed.

Above all, keep challenging yourself to learn and grow. Just like with meditation, you will get distracted, feel like you've fallen off the wagon, or let yourself down. And just like with meditation, you can always begin again.

# RESOURCES

**Andrew Kukes Foundation for Social Anxiety (akfsa.org)**
This website focuses on the education, diagnosis, and treatment of social anxiety.

**Anxiety & Depression Association of America (adaa.org)**
The Anxiety & Depression Association of America is a great resource for up-to-date information about various anxiety and mood disorders.

**The Anxiety Coach (anxietycoach.com)**
David Carbonell is an expert in anxiety disorders. On this website, he provides various tools, education, and resources for different anxiety-related issues.

**Inclusive Therapists (inclusivetherapists.com)**
This is a directory where you can search for therapists in your area. You can search by several different factors, including cultural background, language, spiritual affiliation, and other types of identities.

**National Alliance on Mental Illness (nami.org)**
The National Alliance on Mental Illness provides advocacy, education, and support. You can find support groups, ways to get involved in advocacy, and treatment options on this website.

**Self-Compassion (self-compassion.org)**
This is the website of Kristin Neff, PhD, and it provides research, activities, and resources on the practice of self-compassion.

**TherapyDen (therapyden.com)**
This is a directory where you can search for therapists in your area, including filters for therapist specialty and types of insurance accepted.

**UCLA Mindful Awareness Research Center (uclahealth.org/marc)**
The UCLA Mindful Awareness Research Center provides free meditations, classes, and research about meditation.

### InsightTimer (insighttimer.com)

This is my favorite app for meditation because it is the most diverse and accessible. It currently has 600,000 meditations, all available for free. You can search meditations by length or topic and bookmark your favorite meditations or follow the meditation leaders themselves.

### One Deep Breath (onedeepbreath.io)

This is an app that teaches you science-based breathing exercises. It includes customizable reminders, various breathing techniques, and features to track your breathing practice. It tailors your breathing exercises based on goals you identify.

### Sanvello (sanvello.com)

This is an app that will help you target different aspects of your mental health. It provides mental health education, meditations, coping techniques, and prompts to support your mental wellness.

## BOOKS

*CBT for Anxiety: A Step-by-Step Training Manual for the Treatment of Fear, Panic, Worry, and OCD* by Kimberly Morrow and Elizabeth Dupont Spencer

*Mastery of Your Anxiety and Panic: Workbook,* 4th ed. by David H. Barlow and Michelle G. Craske

*The Mindful Self-Compassion Workbook: A Proven Way to Accept Yourself, Build Inner Strength, and Thrive* by Kristin Neff and Christopher Germer

*Mindsight: The New Science of Personal Transformation* by Daniel J. Siegel

*The Panic Attacks Workbook: A Guided Program for Beating the Panic Trick,* 2nd ed. by David Carbonell

*Rewire Your Anxious Brain: How to Use the Neuroscience of Fear to End Anxiety, Panic, and Worry* by Catherine M. Pittman and Elizabeth M. Karle

*When Panic Attacks: The New, Drug-Free Anxiety Therapy That Can Change Your Life* by David D. Burns

*Why Zebras Don't Get Ulcers,* 3rd ed. by Robert M. Sapolsky

## PODCASTS

*The Panic Pod* by Joshua Fletcher, psychotherapist, and cohost Ella Jean

*Your Anxiety Toolkit: It's a Beautiful Day to Do Hard Things* by Kimberley Quinlan, licensed marriage and family therapist

## OTHER RESOURCES

*The Anti-Anxiety Notebook* (Therapy Notebooks, 2020)—This is a journal with useful prompts and tips to help you understand and cope with anxiety.

National Suicide Prevention Lifeline: 800-273-8255 (TALK)

OCD and Anxiety (YouTube channel)

Therapy in a Nutshell (YouTube channel)

# REFERENCES

Amabile, Teresa A., and Steven J. Kramer. May 6, 2011. "The Power of Small Wins." *Harvard Business Review*. Accessed March 13, 2022. hbr.org/2011/05/the-power -of-small-wins.

American Psychiatric Association. *Diagnostic and Statistical Manual of Mental Disorders, 5th ed.: DSM-5*. Washington, DC: American Psychiatric Association, 2013.

American Psychological Association. "Emotion." *APA Dictionary of Psychology*. Accessed January 29, 2022. dictionary.apa.org/emotion.

Andrews, Gavin, Mark Creamer, Rocco Crino, Caroline Hunt, Lisa Lampe, and Andrew Page. *The Treatment of Anxiety Disorders: Clinician's Guide and Patient Manuals*. New York: Cambridge University Press, 1994.

Anxiety and Depression Association of America. "Facts & Statistics." ADAA.org. Accessed April 11, 2022. adaa.org/understanding-anxiety/facts-statistics.

Bandelow, Borwin, Sophie Michaelis, and Dirk Wedekind. "Treatment of Anxiety Disorders." *Dialogues in Clinical Neuroscience* 19, no. 2 (2017): 93–107. doi.org/10.31887 /dcns.2017.19.2/bbandelow.

Bandura, Albert. "Self-Efficacy." In *The Corsini Encyclopedia of Psychology*, edited by I. B. Weiner and W. E. Craighead. New York: John Wiley & Sons, Inc., 2010. doi.org/10.1002/9780470479216.corpsy0836.

Barlow, David H. and Michelle G. Craske. *Mastery of Your Anxiety and Panic: Workbook*, 4th ed. New York: Oxford University Press, 2006.

Barnard, Laura K. and John F. Curry. "Self-Compassion: Conceptualizations, Correlates, & Interventions." *Review of General Psychology* 15, no. 4 (December 1, 2011): 289–303. doi.org/10.1037/a0025754.

Berenz, Erin C., Timothy P. York, Hanaan Bing-Canar, Ananda B. Amstadter, Briana Mezuk, Charles O. Gardner, & Roxann Roberson-Nay. "Time Course of Panic Disorder and Posttraumatic Stress Disorder Onsets." *Social Psychiatry and Psychiatric Epidemiology*, 54, no. 5 (July 12, 2018): 639–647. doi.org/10.1007/s00127-018-1559-1.

Breines, Juliana G. and Serena Chen. "Self-Compassion Increases Self-Improvement Motivation." *Personality and Social Psychology Bulletin* 38, no. 9 (May 29, 2012): 1133–1143. doi.org/10.1177/0146167212445599.

Broman-Fulks, Joshua J. and Katelyn M. Storey. "Evaluation of a Brief Aerobic Exercise Intervention for High Anxiety Sensitivity." *Anxiety, Stress, & Coping* 21, no. 2 (March 18, 2008): 117–128. doi.org/10.1080/10615800701762675.

Burns, David D. *When Panic Attacks: The New, Drug-Free Anxiety Therapy That Can Change Your Life.* New York: Morgan Road Books, 2006.

Cackovic, Curt, Saad Nazir, and Raman Marwaha. "Panic Disorder." StatPearls. Updated February 7, 2022. ncbi.nlm.nih.gov/books/NBK430973.

Carlson, Linda E., Michael Speca, Kamala D. Patel, and Eileen Goodey. "Mindfulness-Based Stress Reduction in Relation to Quality of Life, Mood, Symptoms of Stress, and Immune Parameters in Breast and Prostate Cancer Outpatients." *Psychosomatic Medicine* 65, no. 4 (July 2003): 571–581. doi.org/10.1097/01.psy.0000074003 .35911.41.

Chau, Lily S. and Roberto Galvez. "Amygdala's Involvement in Facilitating Associative Learning-Induced Plasticity: A Promiscuous Role for the Amygdala in Memory Acquisition." *Frontiers in Integrative Neuroscience* 6 (October 10, 2012): 92. doi.org/10.3389/fnint.2012.00092.

Cleveland Clinic. "Panic Disorder." Last reviewed August 12, 2020. my.clevelandclinic .org/health/diseases/4451-panic-disorder.

Craske, Michelle G. and David H. Barlow. *Mastery of Your Anxiety and Worry: Workbook,* 2nd ed. New York: Oxford University Press, 2006.

Craske, Michelle G., Michael Treanor, Christopher C. Conway, Tomislav Zbozinek, and Bram Vervliet. "Maximizing Exposure Therapy: An Inhibitory Learning Approach." *Behaviour Research and Therapy* 58 (July 2014): 10–23. doi.org/10.1016/j.brat.2014 .04.006.

DeBoer, Lindsey B., Mark B. Powers, Angela C. Utschig, Michael W. Otto, and Jasper A. J. Smits. "Exploring Exercise as an Avenue for the Treatment of Anxiety Disorders." *Expert Review of Neurotherapeutics* 12, no. 8 (2012): 1011–1022. doi.org/10.1586 /ern.12.73.

Desbordes, Gaëlle, Lobsang T. Negi, Thaddeus W. W. Pace, B. Allan Wallace, Charles L. Raison, and Eric L. Schwartz. "Effects of Mindful-Attention and Compassion Meditation Training on Amygdala Response to Emotional Stimuli in an Ordinary, Non-meditative State." *Frontiers in Human Neuroscience* 6 (November 1, 2012): 292. doi.org/10.3389/fnhum.2012.00292.

Dunne, Sarah, David Sheffield, and Joseph Chilcot. "Brief Report: Self-Compassion, Physical Health and the Mediating Role of Health-Promoting Behaviours." *Journal of Health Psychology* 23, no. 7 (April 26, 2016): 993–999. doi.org/10.1177/1359105316643377.

Farb, Norman A. S., Zindel V. Segal, Helen Mayberg, Jim Bean, Deborah McKeon, Zainab Fatima, and Adam K. Anderson. "Attending to the Present: Mindfulness Meditation Reveals Distinct Neural Modes of Self-Reference." *Social Cognitive and Affective Neuroscience* 2, no. 4 (December 2007): 313–322. doi: 10.1093/scan/nsm030.

Fiorella, Logan, and Richard E. Mayer. "The Relative Benefits of Learning by Teaching and Teaching Expectancy." *Contemporary Educational Psychology* 38, no. 4 (October 2013): 281–288. doi.org/10.1016/j.cedpsych.2013.06.001.

Foa, Edna, Elizabeth Hembree, Barbara Olasov Rothbaum, and Sheila Rauch. *Prolonged Exposure Therapy for PTSD: Emotional Processing of Traumatic Experiences: Therapist Guide*, 2nd ed. New York: Oxford University Press, 2019.

Frey, Rebecca J. "Panic Disorder." In *The Gale Encyclopedia of Senior Health: A Guide for Seniors and Their Caregivers*, edited by B. Narins, 3rd ed., vol. 4: 1810–1813. Farmington Hills, Mich.: Gale, 2022. link.gale.com/apps/doc/CX8080300536/HWRC?u=lapl&sid=bookmark-HWRC&xid=2c6a5ffe.

Germer, Christopher and Kristin Neff. *Teaching the Mindful Self-Compassion Program: A Guide for Professionals*, 1st ed. New York: The Guilford Press, 2019.

Gerritsen, Roderik J. S. and Guido P. H. Band. "Breath of Life: The Respiratory Vagal Stimulation Model of Contemplative Activity." *Frontiers in Human Neuroscience* 12 (October 9, 2018): 397. doi.org/10.3389/fnhum.2018.00397.

Goldstein, Andrea N., Stephanie M. Greer, Jared M. Saletin, Allison G. Harvey, Jack B. Nitschke, and Matthew P. Walker. "Tired and Apprehensive: Anxiety Amplifies the Impact of Sleep Loss on Aversive Brain Anticipation." *The Journal of Neuroscience* 33, no. 26 (June 26, 2013): 10607–10615. doi.org/10.1523/jneurosci.5578-12.2013.

Grant, Bridget F., Deborah S. Hasin, Frederick S. Stinson, Deborah A. Dawson, Rise B. Goldstein, Sharon Smith, Boji Huang, and Tulshi D. Saha. "The Epidemiology of DSM-IV Panic Disorder and Agoraphobia in the United States: Results from the National Epidemiologic Survey on Alcohol and Related Conditions." *The Journal of Clinical Psychiatry* 67, no. 3 (March 2006): 363–374. doi.org/10.4088/jcp.v67n0305.

Greenberger, Dennis and Christine A. Padesky. *Mind Over Mood: Change How You Feel by Changing the Way You Think,* 2nd ed. New York: The Guilford Press, 2016.

Ham, Peter, David B. Waters, and M. Norman Oliver. "Treatment of Panic Disorder." *American Family Physician.* February 15, 2005. aafp.org/afp/2005/0215/p733.html.

Hettema, John M., Michael C. Neale, and Kenneth S. Kendler. "A Review and Meta-Analysis of the Genetic Epidemiology of Anxiety Disorders." *American Journal of Psychiatry* 158, no. 10 (October 1, 2001): 1568–1578. doi.org/10.1176/appi.ajp.158.10.1568.

Hofmann, Stefan G., Alice T. Sawyer, Ashley A. Witt, and Diana Oh. "The Effect of Mindfulness-Based Therapy on Anxiety and Depression: A Meta-Analytic Review." *Journal of Consulting and Clinical Psychology* 78, no. 2 (April 1, 2010): 156–168. doi.org/10.1037/a0018555.

Hyman, Bruce M. and Cherry Pedrick. *The OCD Workbook: Your Guide to Breaking Free from Obsessive-Compulsive Disorder*, 3rd ed. Oakland, Calif.: New Harbinger Publications, 2010.

Johnson, Jon. "What to Know about Diaphragmatic Breathing." *Medical News Today.* Accessed February 5, 2022. medicalnewstoday.com/articles/diaphragmatic-breathing#additional-treatments.

Kalmbach, David A., Yu Fang, J. Todd Arnedt, Amy L. Cochran, Patricia J. Deldin, Adam I. Kaplin, and Srijan Sen. "Effects of Sleep, Physical Activity, and Shift Work on Daily Mood: A Prospective Mobile Monitoring Study of Medical Interns." *Journal of General Internal Medicine* 33, no. 6 (March 14, 2018): 914–920. doi.org/10.1007/s11606-018-4373-2.

Kessler, Ronald C., Wai Tat Chiu, Robert Jin, Ayelet Meron Ruscio, Katherine Shear, and Ellen E. Walters. "The Epidemiology of Panic Attacks, Panic Disorder, and Agoraphobia in the National Comorbidity Survey Replication." *Archives of General Psychiatry* 63, no. 4 (April 2006): 415–424. doi.org/10.1001/archpsyc.63.4.415.

Larson, Emily R. and Christine A. Adamec. "Panic Disorder." In *The Gale Encyclopedia of Genetic Disorders,* edited by B. Narins, 5th ed., vol. 3: 1439–1443. Farmington Hills, Mich.: Gale, 2022. link.gale.com/apps/doc/CX8289300427/HWRC?u=lapl&sid=bookmark-HWRC&xid=4842c457.

Lieberman, Matthew D., Naomi I. Eisenberger, Molly J. Crockett, Sabrina M. Tom, Jennifer H. Pfeifer, and Baldwin M. Way. "Putting Feelings into Words." *Psychological Science* 18, no. 5 (May 1, 2007): 421–428. doi.org/10.1111/j.1467-9280.2007.01916.x.

Luders, Eileen, Florian Kurth, Emeran A. Mayer, Arthur W. Toga, Katherine L. Narr, and Christian Gaser. "The Unique Brain Anatomy of Meditation Practitioners: Alterations in Cortical Gyrification." *Frontiers in Human Neuroscience* 6 (February 29, 2012): 34. doi.org/10.3389/fnhum.2012.00034.

Mayo Clinic Staff. "Depersonalization-Derealization Disorder." MayoClinic.org. Accessed February 12, 2022. mayoclinic.org/diseases-conditions/depersonalization-derealization-disorder/symptoms-causes/syc-20352911.

Meuret, Alicia E., Michael P. Twohig, David Rosenfield, Steven C. Hayes, and Michelle G. Craske. "Brief Acceptance and Commitment Therapy and Exposure for Panic Disorder: A Pilot Study." *Cognitive and Behavioral Practice* 19, no. 4 (November 2012): 606–618. doi.org/10.1016/j.cbpra.2012.05.004.

Moore, Catherine. "Positive Daily Affirmations: Is There Science Behind It?" PositivePsychology.com. March 4, 2019. positivepsychology.com/daily-affirmations.

Morrow, Kimberly and Elizabeth DuPont Spencer. "CBT for Anxiety and OCD: Everything You Need to Know to Provide a Successful Treatment [online course]." Accessed April 12, 2022. anxietytraining.com/online-courses-for-mental-professionals-school-districts-and-individual-clinicians/cbt-for-anxiety-and-ocd-everything-you-need-to-know-to-provide-successful-treatment.

National Alliance on Mental Illness. "Anxiety Disorders." NAMI.org. Reviewed December 2017. nami.org/about-mental-illness/mental-health-conditions/anxiety-disorders/treatment.

National Center for Complementary and Integrative Health. "Meditation: In Depth." Last updated April 2016. nccih.nih.gov/health/meditation-in-depth#hed3.

Rimmele, Ulrike, Bea Costa Zellweger, Bernard Marti, Roland Seiler, Changiz Mohiyeddini, Ulrike Ehlert, and Markus Heinrichs. "Trained Men Show Lower Cortisol, Heart Rate and Psychological Responses to Psychosocial Stress Compared with Untrained Men." *Psychoneuroendocrinology* 32, no. 6 (June 8, 2007): 627–635. doi.org/10.1016/j.psyneuen.2007.04.005.

Rosenbaum, Jerrold F. "Limited-Symptom Panic Attacks: Missed and Masked Diagnosis." *Psychosomatics* 28, no. 8 (August 1987): 407–408, 411–412. doi.org/10.1016/s0033-3182(87)72491-8.

Rosenberg, Joan I. *90 Seconds to a Life You Love: How to Master Your Difficult Feelings to Cultivate Lasting Confidence, Resilience, and Authenticity.* New York: Little, Brown Spark, 2020.

Sansone, Randy A. and Lori A. Sansone. "Gratitude and Well Being: The Benefits of Appreciation." *Psychiatry* 7, no. 11 (November 2010): 18–22. psycnet.apa.org/record/2010-25532-003.

Sapolsky, Robert M. *Why Zebras Don't Get Ulcers.* Old Saybrook, Conn.: Tantor Audio, 2012. Audiobook, unabridged ed.

Shapiro, Shauna L., Kirk Warren Brown, and Gina M. Biegel. "Teaching Self-Care to Caregivers: Effects of Mindfulness-Based Stress Reduction on the Mental Health of Therapists in Training." *Training and Education in Professional Psychology* 1, no. 2 (May 2007): 105–115. doi.org/10.1037/1931-3918.1.2.105.

Siegel, Daniel J. "Mindfulness Training and Neural Integration: Differentiation of Distinct Streams of Awareness and the Cultivation of Well-Being." *Social Cognitive and Affective Neuroscience* 2, no. 4 (December 1, 2007): 259–263. doi.org/10.1093/scan/nsm034.

Smeets, Elke, Kristin Neff, Hugo Alberts, and Madelon Peters. "Meeting Suffering with Kindness: Effects of a Brief Self-Compassion Intervention for Female College Students." *Journal of Clinical Psychology*, 70, no. 9 (April 1, 2014): 794–807. doi.org/10.1002/jclp.22076.

Speca, Michael, Linda E. Carlson, Eileen Goodey, and Maureen Angen. "A Randomized, Wait-List Controlled Clinical Trial: The Effect of a Mindfulness Meditation-Based Stress Reduction Program on Mood and Symptoms of Stress in Cancer Outpatients." *Psychosomatic Medicine* 62, no. 5 (September–October 2000): 613–622. doi.org/10.1097/00006842-200009000-00004.

Strauss, Clara, Billie Lever Taylor, Jenny Gu, Willem Kuyken, Ruth Baerd, Fergal Jones, and Kate Cavanagh. "What Is Compassion and How Can We Measure It? A Review of Definitions and Measures." *Clinical Psychology Review* 47 (July 2016): 15–27. doi.org/10.1016/j.cpr.2016.05.004.

Swain, Jessica, Karen Hancock, Cassandra Hainsworth, and Jenny Bowman. "Acceptance and Commitment Therapy in the Treatment of Anxiety: A Systematic Review." *Clinical Psychology Review* 33, no. 8 (December 2013): 965–978. doi.org/10.1016/j.cpr.2013.07.002.

Vandergriendt, Carly. "Treating Panic Attack Disorder." Healthline.com. Last updated August 25, 2021. healthline.com/health/panic-attack-medication#panic-attack-medication-list.

Walsh, Roger and Shauna L. Shapiro. "The Meeting of Meditative Disciplines and Western Psychology: A Mutually Enriching Dialogue." *American Psychologist* 61, no. 3 (2006): 227–239. doi.org/10.1037/0003-066x.61.3.227.

Webb, Christian A., Courtney Beard, Sarah J. Kertz, Kean J. Hsu, and Thröstur Björgvinsson. "Differential Role of CBT Skills, DBT Skills and Psychological Flexibility in Predicting Depressive versus Anxiety Symptom Improvement." *Behaviour Research and Therapy*, 81 (June 2016): 12–20. doi.org/10.1016/j.brat.2016.03.006.

Wegner, Daniel M., David J. Schneider, Samuel R. Carter, and Teri L. White. "Paradoxical Effects of Thought Suppression." *Journal of Personality and Social Psychology* 53, no. 1 (July 1987): 5–13. doi.org/10.1037/0022-3514.53.1.5.

Winerman, Lea. "Suppressing the 'White Bears'." *Monitor on Psychology* 42, no. 9 (October 2011): 44–45. apa.org/monitor/2011/10/unwanted-thoughts.

Wolf, Christiane and J. Greg Serpa. *A Clinician's Guide to Teaching Mindfulness*, 1st ed. Oakland, Calif.: New Harbinger Publications, 2015.

Zucker, Bonnie. "Panic Attacks: A Brief Intervention." Simple Practice Learning. Video, 61:00. Accessed April 12, 2022. simplepracticelearning.com/courses/panic-attacks-brief-intervention.

# INDEX

# About the Author

**Mayra Diaz, MS, LMFT,** is a licensed marriage and family therapist specializing in anxiety and OCD and working with the Black, Indigenous People of Color (BIPOC) community. She completed a bachelor of arts in psychology at the University of California, Santa Barbara, and a master of science in counseling at California State University, Northridge. Mayra is certified in cognitive behavioral therapy (CBT) and trained in exposure and response prevention (ERP). She has a private practice in Los Angeles, California. She challenges her clients and actively promotes their learning so they can feel ownership of their own change. For more information about Mayra, visit her website at MayraDiazTherapy.com.

CPSIA information can be obtained
at www.ICGtesting.com
Printed in the USA
LVHW071955190722
723880LV00015B/532

9 781638 077954